WOW GOD!

TRUE LIFE SPIRITUAL ADVENTURES
OF MISSIONARIES

Richard & Sheryl Boettiger

Harvest Creek Publishing

CONROE, TEXAS

Unless otherwise noted, Scriptures are taken from *The New International Version* of The Holy Bible (NIV).

Scripture quotations marked (NKJV) are taken from the *New King James Version.* Copyright © 1979, 1980, 1982 by Thomas Nelson, Inc., Publishers.

Richard & Sheryl Boettiger/Harvest Creek Publishing
9303 East Lakeside Drive
Magnolia, Texas 77354
www. Boettigerministries.org

Cover and Book Layout ©2021 Harvest Creek Design

Ordering Information:

Quantity sales. Special discounts are available on quantity purchases by corporations, associations, and others. For details, please contact teresa@harvestcreek.net.

Wow God! —2nd ed.

ISBN 978-1-7373567-1-4

INTRODUCTION

Reading "Wow God!" is like reading the Book of Acts, the actions of the Apostles. These exciting stories, lived out in faith by Pastors Richard and Sheryl Boettiger, are true life adventures they experienced through fifty years of ministry.

Each chapter is truly an adventure of faith, as they prayerfully follow the leading of the Holy Spirit and witness God's faithfulness over and over again. They witnessed the miracles of countless young men and women who came to know Jesus, the glorious financial provision at just the right moment, and the favor of God turning obstacles into opportunities for His glory.

Through the entire book, you sense their optimistic dependence on God's faithfulness, and you can feel their excitement during each adventure!

It has been my honor and distinct pleasure to be a part of this publication. I know that it will expand your faith and give you a new level of assurance, that where God guides you, He will provide.

Larry G. Langston
Heaven's Breath Publications

TABLE OF CONTENTS

CHAPTER 1

ADVENTURES WITH THE LOVE OF MY LIFE

God made you. God made me.
Then He whispered, "Meant to be."

IT ALL BEGAN when our eyes locked through the kitchen window in 1956. I was 16, and Sheryl was 11. I was painting the outside of the window, and Sheryl was washing dishes when that life-changing moment happened! We sensed that God had something incredibly special for our lives together.

We regularly had "testimony time" in our University Assembly of God Church in Waxahachie, Texas. Without fail, Sheryl would stand up and tell how much she loved the Lord and what he had done for her. At the end of every testimony, she would quote Nehemiah 8:10, *"The joy of the Lord is my strength."* That, coupled with her vivacious smile, just lit up my heart. I remember telling myself, "I want to live my life with that joyful girl."

The next few years brought many changes to our lives. First, Sheryl became the social butterfly both in high school and in college. Then, God called her into the ministry, and she became the youngest credential holder in the North Texas District of the Assemblies of God at age 14. Sheryl was active in holding revivals and ministry on the weekends.

I graduated from high school from Southwestern. Then, I went on to graduate from the Northrop Institute of Technology in California. After that, Sheryl and I kept in touch and dated whenever I was in town. But then, the epic moment happened again.

...socially, I was the complete opposite of Sheryl.

During a visit to our hometown in Waxahachie, Texas, I asked Sheryl for a date. The bells and whistles all went off spontaneously, and we were engaged shortly after that. I was 21, and she was 16.

We were immediately reminded by parents and friends of the social, and perhaps spiritual, distance between us. Though I was a Christian, socially, I was the complete opposite of Sheryl. Growing up, I was the lone motorcycle rider in our small town. So it was no wonder why Sheryl's parents were concerned.

Enter the Holy Spirit's guidance per Jeremiah 29:11, "*for I know the plans I have for you says the Lord. Plans for peace and not for evil, to give you a future and a hope.*" While desperately praying and fasting, God spontaneously gave Sheryl this song—both the text and the music—as she sat down at the piano:

GOD MADE YOU FOR ME

God made you for me, that together His will we might see
That all our days would be happy and gay
For God made you for me.
Our love is true that we know
And to others our love we will show
For our love is pure gold
And will never grow old for God made you for me
All of our dreams He'll fulfill as we climb on earth's highest hill
And the rest of our days, we will offer our praise
To the one who made you for me
Our wedding day is here, and the Lord is standing near
For the Lord, He ordained that we come in His name
For He made you for me
God made you for me

When Sheryl sang this song from memory to her parents, they were amazed and convinced that God had spoken a clear word about our love for each other. On May 25, 1963, we were married at the University Assembly of God Church in Waxahachie, with five hundred teachers, ministers, and fellow students in attendance. It was a beautiful wedding with Pastor Joe Adams and Dr. Harrison officiating.

And it was the beginning of our extraordinary adventures together with the Lord.

REFLECTIONS:

Have you ever experienced a life-changing moment in your life? A moment where you knew, without a doubt, that God had something extraordinary for you? These "God moments" can be so profound and transformative that there is no denying it was the Lord's hand in that experience.

God moments happen when it is clear that He has intervened and miraculously shown Himself. We must appreciate these special times and acknowledge that it was the Lord. Recall a time when you felt the overwhelming power of God's presence in a simple moment.

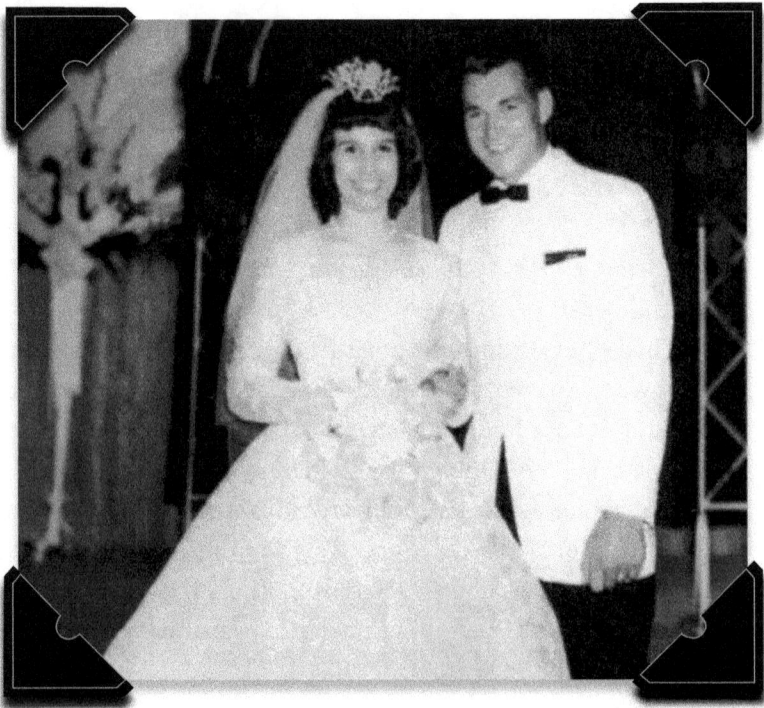

Mr. and Mrs. Richard Boettiger, married May 25, 1963

CHAPTER 2

OUR FIRST
APARTMENT

---

*Delight yourself in the Lord, and He will
give you the desires of your heart.*

Psalm 37:4

I WAS IN THE NAVY and stationed temporarily in San Francisco, California. Our ship, the guided-missile cruiser USS Topeka, was moving back to our home base in Long Beach in just one month. We were given only three days of leave to find an apartment there before re-boarding the ship to head out for sea trials.

The first day was taken up by travel from San Francisco to Long Beach, then browsing through apartment ads and finding a motel. Early the following day, we located a wonderful newly furnished apartment in a friendly, safe neighborhood on Magnolia Avenue, right there in Long Beach.

This would be the perfect place for my bride of only one month. The only problem was we could not begin to afford it on my salary of a mere $183.10 per month. So, we continued to search all day, and by the evening, we were desperate and frantic. The apartments we could afford were roach-infested, dirty, and located in undesirable locations. I pulled the car over, and we both cried out to God, with tears flowing down our faces.

The next day, I had to take the bus back to San Francisco or be considered AWOL from the Navy! This was our "Red Sea" experience. While we were desperately praying, a lady tapped on the window.

Naturally, we were startled and embarrassed. The lady said, "Are you still looking for an apartment?"

It was then we recognized her as the landlord of the first beautiful apartment we have viewed. We had no idea that we had pulled over, directly across the street from her apartment. Of all the locations in Long Beach, God had directed us there.

We were awestruck at God's "over the top" provision for us!

Tearfully, we explained that we were still looking, and she said, "If you are handy, I'll make you a good deal."

We gladly agreed to do light maintenance and moved our meager belongings, which amounted to Sheryl's clothing, personal items, and the wedding gifts that had been given to us just one month prior. We were awestruck at God's "over the top" provision for us!

That fantastic apartment was used to befriend and minister to many of my sailor peers. They would look around and say, "How do you afford this beautiful apartment?" Of course, to God's glory, we always shared the testimony of how the Lord had directed us to that apartment.

Sheryl continued to work on her undergraduate degree, and Jen, our landlady, became friends with Sheryl. Jen was so gracious to her during my long absences at sea. We were also very active in ministry to the military personnel in our local church, pastored by Rev. Buntain.

REFLECTIONS:

Finding a place to live in a new city can be stressful. And when there is a time-crunch involved, it can be downright agonizing! But the Lord cares about every detail of your life, including where you live. He wants to position you in the right community and near the perfect neighbors for His glory.

Have you experienced the hand of God directing your steps when it came to choosing a place to settle? Thank Him now for opening and closing doors for you to be planted in just the right locale.

CHAPTER 3

GOD'S DIVINE GUIDANCE FOR OUR MOVE TO TULSA, OKLAHOMA

In all your ways, acknowledge Him, and He will direct your paths.

Proverbs 3:6

SHORTLY BEFORE MY DISCHARGE FROM THE NAVY, Sheryl and I prayed for the Lord to guide us on where we should move to begin our new life together. One evening, Sheryl had a vision of an unusual church. The wall separating the foyer from the sanctuary was entirely glass. She saw the entire church setting, placement of piano and organ, and other details in one split second. As she shared this vision with me, we each felt we should have the Navy move our household goods to Tulsa, Oklahoma. Bear in mind, we did not know anyone in Tulsa!

However, when we ultimately moved to Tulsa and entered this church, we immediately recognized it as the one in Sheryl's vision. Missionary Charles Greenaway preached powerful mission sermons in this church that led to my call to full-time ministry.

OUR VIRGIN INDIAN LAND IN HIDDEN VALLEY

Isaiah 12:3, *"Therefore, you will joyously draw water from the springs of salvation."*

We bought some land out in the country, intending to build our dream house. I bought a dilapidated water well drilling rig, and we drilled several dry holes with great disappointment. We purchased some dynamite, all to no avail; there was no water on our new land.

The property would be worthless if we could not get water. So, Sheryl suggested we pray about exactly where to drill. I was skeptical, thinking God was not concerned about such earthly things as water wells. Yet, we were desperate.

I humbled myself, and we prayed for guidance. Sheryl then pointed to a spot about seven feet away. She said, "God is telling me we should drill here." So I moved the drilling rig, and at twenty feet down, I hit a strong water vein. From that moment on, we never ran out of water.

Sheryl watered her large garden of green beans, which also provided an abundance of potatoes, peas, and other vegetables for our pastor and church friends. In addition, she planted gardenias and roses all around our yard. And, we had plenty of well water! This provision and direction from God made a great impression that He cares about everything in our lives.

made a great impression that He cares about everything in our lives.

SHERYL LOSES HER HAIR – ALOPECIA

Psalm 103:3, *"The Lord forgives all your sins and heals all your diseases."*

One day Sheryl noticed a bald spot on her head. Over the next few days, that spot grew exponentially. We went to a specialist and tried everything they suggested, all to no avail.

The doctors were baffled, and Sheryl was horrified. She began intensely going through the Word, writing down all the scriptures on healing. She fasted and prayed earnestly. Finally, God told her to go to the door and look at the trees. It was late Fall, and the trees were bare.

God said, "Who puts the leaves back on the trees?"

Sheryl said, "You do, Lord."

God said, "I will put hair back on your head." And He did just that. Sheryl now has an extra thick head of hair.

The Lord reserves the right to test and grow our faith. Our faith for healing was tested many times in later years, and we always related back to this experience. God was preparing us for faith adventures with him.

The Lord reserves the right to test and grow our faith.

REFLECTIONS:

The Bible says that faith is something that is built within us. The way our faith is strengthened is by putting it to the test. Someone once characterized faith as a muscle. You must stretch it and use it often to develop it into something substantial.

CHAPTER 4

WHERE YOUR TREASURE IS, THERE WILL YOUR HEART BE

Choose this day whom you will serve.

Joshua 24:15

WE HAD OUR FIRST CHILD, a whopping eleven-pound boy we named Ricky. Then fourteen months later, our daughter Sharla was born. Life was good; we were busy in our local church. At that time, I served as the Sunday School Superintendent and also had an excellent paying job working for McDonald Douglas as a machinist. We had plans drawn up for our dream home.

God began to deal with us about full-time ministry, although I was resistant. Unbeknownst to me, Sheryl was fasting and praying while I was at work. I remember lying on the couch with my head on her lap, telling her about the beautiful house we would build in our scenic setting called "Hidden Valley."

She blurted out, "This is not what I want; I want to serve God full time." Her comment left me furious—feeling rejected, demeaned, and slighted.

The next day at work, God spoke to me in a gentle, loving way, and I found myself weeping and listening *I was resisting God's call on my life.* to God. In God's providence, Sheryl met an on-fire for God couple, Brenda and Sonny Sumner. They were Methodists and had received the Baptism in the Holy Spirit.

Sonny and Brenda hosted prayer meetings in their home, where God did many miracles of healing. Sonny told me that he would do anything if God would call them into ministry. This shamed and challenged me as I was resisting God's call on my life.

Later that year, Sonny left his high-paying position at American Airlines and attended Southwestern Assemblies of God University. He and I held some tent meetings, and we became sanitation engineers, hauling the trash for the college in exchange for our tuition. Both of us finished school debt-free! We learned that sometimes the lowly jobs are God's provision. The Sumners, along with their family, have spent their entire lives as missionaries in Central America.

MY CALLING AND BIBLE SCHOOL

Isaiah 30:21, *"You shall hear a voice behind you saying, 'This is the way, walk in it."*

Veteran missionary Charles Greenaway came to our church in Tulsa to preach a Mission Convention. He spoke many memorable teachings like, "It's not the cross that should bother you, it's the absence of the cross, because Jesus said,

'Take up your cross and follow me.' Charles also said, 'Go ahead and lay up treasures for your children, and when you die, they will fight over them, but when you lay up treasures in heaven, they will rise up and call you blessed.'

After several evenings, I found myself at the altar in complete submission to God's call. The next day at work, I arranged for a one-year leave of absence from my job. Sheryl left right away with our two children to enroll me in all Bible courses and attend the initial classes. I arrived two weeks later, not knowing just what the future held (hence the leave of absence) to begin attending class. Our daughter, Sharla, had been very sick from the time of her birth. On the day we came to Bible School, God totally healed her.

While volunteering at our Assemblies of God Orphans' Home, we were placed in charge of nineteen boys every weekend. I repaired bikes, washing machines, mowers, toys—you name it, which kept me very busy. Sheryl cut hair, cooked, cleaned, etc., for our little unit of nineteen boys.

Once in a very moving Sunday Service there at the children's home, God spoke to me in an audible voice. It was directly behind me and entirely perceptible. God said, "I want you to preach my Word."

Frightened yet awestruck, I collapsed into the pew, grabbed my Bible, and said, "God, if this is you, show me in your Word."

With one quick movement, I opened my Bible and landed on II Timothy 4:2. That passage reads: "Preach the Word; be ready in season and out of season, reprove, rebuke and exhort with all patience and teaching."

I was shaken and fearful about how I would provide for my family in what was, to me, a totally foreign environment. Sheryl was thrilled beyond words, as her deepest desire for the future had been answered. God had spoken!

REFLECTIONS:

There are times in life when God sees the bigger picture for us. We may have reached a place where we are comfortable and happy with what we have accomplished. But the Lord has a greater goal for us to obtain. God never wants us to settle or become satisfied with the status quo.

Reflect on a time where you struggled with a change that the Lord wanted you to make. What was your greatest fear in accepting His request? Looking back, wasn't God's plan more significant than you could have ever imagined or accomplished on your own?

CHAPTER 5

DIVINE GUIDANCE TO GERMANY

He has made everything beautiful in its appropriate time.

Ecclesiastes 3:11

I FINISHED THE FOUR-YEAR DEGREE PROGRAM in only two and one-half years. It was a taxing but wonderful time of learning to trust God for everything. It was also a forerunner to the faith adventures to come.

Sheryl also finished her degree at Texas Wesleyan University in Ft. Worth, Texas. As graduation approached, my peers would say things like, "God called me to pastor [be an evangelist, be a missionary]," etc. Sheryl and I had not explicitly heard from God, and we were desperately praying for His perfect will.

About three weeks before graduation, Brother Ohlin from the Assemblies of God Mobilization and Placement Service spoke in our chapel at Southwestern. He outlined two desperate needs of the ministry. One was in Germany. Unbeknownst to me, Sheryl had received a call to Germany at the First Kids Camp of the North Texas District when she was nine years old.

At one of the camp altar services, she was slain in the Spirit and saw a map of Europe with a bold outline and Germany's name. Katy Jean Jones and Betty Savage carried her back to the cabin as she was "in the Spirit of God" for several hours. She had not shared this call with me as she didn't want me to be "wife called."

As we knelt there at Brother Ohlin's service, Sheryl silently prayed for confirmation. God said to us, "You are going to Germany."

Sheryl was joyful beyond belief! We made the commitment that began our first full-time faith venture into the unknown of totally trusting God for absolutely everything.

OUR FIRST FAITH ADVENTURE

Psalm 37:5, *"Commit your way to the Lord, trust also in Him, and He will bring it to pass."*

We obtained our passports by rush order. We sold or gave away everything we owned to our friends at Bible School and headed toward New York. No one knew of our plans, except for immediate family. We did not have the funds for our Trans-Atlantic flight—enter the Holy Spirit's provision.

On the way, we visited Sheryl's brother, Jerry Sturgeon, who was in the U.S. Navy, stationed in Washington D.C. Jerry, along with Pastor Sam Rust, arranged for us to share our vision to go to Germany with a handful of people on Wednesday night. They took a spontaneous Missionary offering for us.

From that Missionary offering, we had just enough for a one-way ticket on Icelandic Airlines to Luxembourg. In the seventies, this was the cheapest flight to Europe. We were surrounded by a plane full of hippies.

When we arrived in Luxembourg, the customs officer confiscated our passports as we had no return ticket and no means of support. He screamed at us to call the U.S. embassy and travel back to America. Our faith was being tested.

Our faith was being tested.

Sheryl had brought her accordion, so we began to sing songs of praise in the airport. The hippies seemed to really enjoy our music. Our four-year-old Ricky and three-year-old Sharla went to sleep on the bench at the airport. We prayed desperate prayers.

At midnight, God spoke to me to go and get our passports. It was a new shift of customs workers, and as I made my request for our documents, the customs officer reached into the top drawer of his desk, produced our passports, stamped them, and gave them to me. We had no idea that a shift change, with no instructions left to hold our passports, enabled the customer officer to provide us with our passports with no strings attached.

As quickly as possible, we purchased tickets to fly to Frankfurt, Germany. We were down to our last two hundred dollars and knew the Frankfurt customs office could also confiscate our passports. However, we were overjoyed when the customs workers there simply stamped our passports and now, we were in Germany!

REFLECTIONS:

God often gives us a vision for our life, but not everyone shares that same dream. In Genesis 37, Joseph had a dream and a vision. But his brothers didn't share that goal. As the "kid brother," they thought he was crazy. But this didn't deter Joseph because his dream wasn't ordinary. It was EXTRA-ordinary—it was God's vision.

Has God given you an idea that was beyond what most people would consider ordinary? Have you trusted the Lord to bring it to pass? Challenge yourself to dare to dream today. Start with God's word and ask Him to open doors that no man can shut.

CHAPTER 6

THE WILL AND THE TIMING OF GOD

Eye has not seen, nor ear heard, nor has it entered into the heart of man the things God has prepared for those who love him. But God has revealed them to us by the Holy Spirit.

1 Corinthians 2:9-10

WE WERE GIVEN THE NAME of Harold and Agnes Schmitt from Brother Ohlin from Mobilization and Placement and had purchased tickets to take a bus to the missionaries' home in Bad Soden. We were waiting for the bus, and when the bus arrived, the Germans pushed ahead of us, leaving us standing with our two small children, with our suitcases. So, we caught the next bus.

We learned to be aggressive and hold our place in line after that! That was a lesson we practiced many times in our 50 years of ministry.

The Schmitts were so thrilled to see us when we arrived at the apartment. They told us they were going to a Missions Convention in Spain. Harold and Agnes were very congenial and asked if we could house-sit and pick up their mail.

It was a lovely apartment on the third floor—what a place God had provided, with a bakery down the street and a German meat store. Our children were so well-behaved and happy. As Harold was going out the door, in a spur of the moment, he wrote down the name of Sgt. Carl Kristener, along with the Sergeant's telephone number. God had provided us a place to stay and a contact person.

GOD PREPARES THE WAY BEFORE US

Isaiah 45:2, *"I will go before you and make the crooked places straight."*

The next day, we bought a train ticket to Mannheim. Our two precious children, Ricky and Sharla, loved the new adventure and exploring the train. Carl was a motor pool sergeant and sent a driver to pick us up at the train station.

Within minutes of meeting Carl and his wife Jackie, we were on our knees praising God. Two weeks before, while we were in Texas hearing God's call, God had spoken to Jackie and Carl that a couple was coming and that they were to help. It was as in Acts 10, where God spoke to Cornelius and then to Peter. As Peter was obedient, God opened a new ministry to the Gentiles.

We visited the Kristeners a few months ago after being apart for forty-five years. We had a wonderful time recounting God's wonderful blessings and provision. Since Carl was the lay Pastor of the Mannheim Assemblies of God serviceman's group, he had many contacts with the ways and means to help us.

First, he arranged for us to get a little Volkswagen hatchback. Upon bringing it back from Mannheim, I took the steps to the third floor up to the Schmitt's apartment. At the same time, Sheryl, Ricky, and Sharla took the elevator down to go and buy some good German cheesecake. When they got to the parking lot, Ricky said, "There's our new car."

Sheryl said, "It can't be; it has green tags," which were U.S. Military tags.

> "The angel said it was our car!"

Ricky said, "Don't you see the angel by the car? He told me it was our car."

I came down about that time and said, "How did you know it was our car?"

Ricky replied, "The angel said it was our car!"

Sheryl and I wept as we were so honored with God's presence and confirmation that we were in His perfect will.

It was a fantastic little car. We used it for several years, carrying up to nine U.S. servicemen in it. We were excited as our faith adventure was taking shape and direction.

GOD'S EARLY PROVISION FOR A PLACE TO LIVE

Luke 6:38, "*Give, and it will be given you a good measure, pressed down, shaken together and running over, will be poured into your lap.*"

As soon as possible, we moved to Hedesheim into one room of Taunta Linda Fetchenhouer's house. She was a precious German lady who had volunteered to help us find a place to live. In 1970, there was at least a six-month waiting period in locating any available space. We had promised her 100 DEMs (Deutsche Marks) a month for the one room.

Every morning, we spent time in urgent prayer for God's leading and then spent time looking for a ministry facility.

One morning we were down to our last 20 DEMs (about five 5 U.S. dollars). I began praising the Lord that He would provide for us. Sheryl was a bit unsettled and took the last 20 DEMs to buy milk and bread for our little ones. I was still praising God when I heard hard knocks on the window.

Carl Kristner drove up to our roadside window; he had me quickly open it up and started unloading a literal truckload of groceries. It seems the Mess Hall Sergeant was getting an inspection and had too much inventory! He asked Carl if he knew anyone who could use the tremendous supply of food.

The list of groceries included: dehydrated steak, dehydrated fish, dehydrated apples, many other dehydrated fruits, flour, sugar, spam, pancake mix, lard, butter, brown sugar, many kinds of cereal, cooking cereal, oatmeal, cookies, and a variety of nuts. Everything was packed in huge containers and was indeed enough to feed an army. It covered the entire floor and furniture. Just as quickly as Carl had come, he was gone.

On the way to the store to buy groceries with our last 20 Deutsche marks, Sheryl heard God say, "Stop complaining, you answered my call, and now trust me for everything." She began praising God for the privilege of serving Him in the land of her calling. Returning home, she entered in split-second timing. Seeing all of those groceries, in wide-eyed bewilderment and amazement, she said, "Where did all this come from?"

Ricky, our four-year-old, jumped up and down, his arms flailing. "Jesus did it. Jesus did it," he said.

Our landlady allowed us to put the enormous supply of God's provision in her basement. That weekend, there was a large gathering of servicemen in Eartshausen, Germany. Sheryl baked six apple pies, one pecan pie, and two pumpkin pies to take to the group.

Philippians 4:19, *"But my God shall supply all your needs, according to His riches in glory by Christ Jesus."*

We were looking for an apartment and place of ministry. God was so gracious to allow us to stay at Taunta Linda's one room. We had agreed to pay 100 DEMs a month, and the rent was due! She did not know we were faith missionaries.

I was praising God, and Sheryl was crying. I said, "God knows our need. Start praising the Lord."

We both joined hands and began thanking God for His divine supply. God spoke to Sheryl, and she looked out the open window and said, "The postman has something for us."

He said, "Richard Boettiger?"

I said, "Ja," and he said, "Sign here."

He gave me 100 DEMs cash. Sheryl shouted out, "Hallelujah, hallelujah!!!"

Every time Sheryl saw the postman after that, he would say to her, "Hallelujah!" Ha! The money was from Klaus Puplickhousen, someone we did not know and had never met.

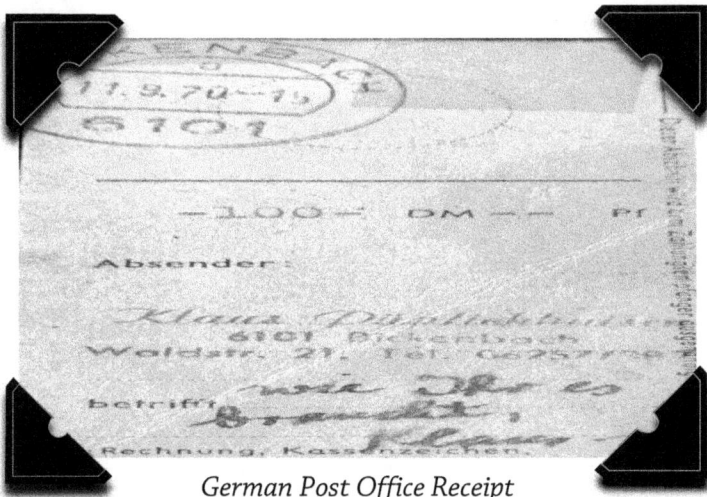

German Post Office Receipt

REFLECTIONS:

Angels minister or serve the children of God. They often act as couriers for the answers to our prayers. The Bible recounts many times when angels brought God's response to the prayers of His people.

They also bring blessings and provisions to us. Angels are active in the world today, even though we can't physically see them. Think about a time in your own life when you felt the tangible presence of God. Could it have been one of His ministering angels at work in your life?

CHAPTER 7

GERMAN KINDERGARTEN FOR OUR SON, RICKY

It is more blessed to give than to receive.

Acts 20:35

TAUNTA LINDA, a wonderful Christian lady, had no children and offered to take Ricky to kindergarten and help him get enrolled. She would take Ricky on her bike and proudly ride him through town to school, where he learned to speak German like the local children.

Little did we know that he was being prepared for his future as a missionary to Germany. Rick, now fifty-two, has been a missionary to Germany for twenty-eight years. It was God's plan that he learned to speak German so young.

In the following years, Taunta Linda graciously cooked for our missions' teams brought from the states. She taught Sheryl how to cook German meals. Great is her reward in Heaven.

GOD'S PROTECTION ON A BORROWED TENT

Psalm 91:2, *"I will say of the Lord, he is my refuge and my fortress, my God in whom I trust."*

Early on, we met a German Pastor, Peter Osmus, who loaned me a tent. We were helping Guntar Kaupp start a local church in Mannheim, and he secured permission to erect that tent in the town marketplace.

A group of young people from America had come to provide the music and help pass out fliers at the tent meeting. Every night, the few German Christians would roll the sides down, so no one could see. We would then roll up the sides and encourage them to let people pass by, seeing the joy of the young people and hearing the Gospel. They were to be a city set on the hill, so all could see!

Next to us was a huge Barnum and Bailey circus tent. One night a fierce storm seemingly came from out of nowhere. We desperately did everything we could to anchor and stabilize our flimsy tent for about three arduous hours. When the storm subsided, the circus tent was destroyed and collapsed on the ground— large poles and all! It was ripped to shreds.

But to our shock and amazement, our little gospel tent had only one small tear in the entrance canopy. God had supernaturally protected us! We continued to hold evangelistic meetings for the rest of the week.

OUR FIRST COFFEE HOUSE IN MANNHEIM

Jeremiah 30:19, *"Out of them will proceed thanksgiving and the voice of them who make merry, and I will multiply them, and they will not be a few."*

One day while on the hunt for a place of ministry, we noticed broken glass in an entry door of a tire store. Word on the street was that the entire block would be torn down to make space for a hospital. The store had moved out early in the month.

We had no money, but the store owner agreed to let us take possession immediately. We proceeded to build a first-class coffee house. It would be the first Christian coffeehouse in Germany, located at J4A2A on the corner of the two busiest main streets downtown.

I found two large wagon wheels and made them into our unique light fixtures in the coffeehouse. It was a striking western-looking chandelier. The young German people found it very interesting that we were from Texas and always asked about the cowboys and our guns!

We also secured the adjacent store, which had previously been an electrical appliance business, and made it into a small apartment for our family. We furnished it with discarded furniture; Germans call it "junking." We would have such fun picking up furniture pieces: a stove, a couch, many things right off the street. We were shopping and buying without money, as stated in Isaiah 55:1. Most of it was pretty nice, too.

We were shopping and buying without money...

Our Family in front of the Coffee House

OUR KEROSENE HEATER BLOWS UP

Genesis 50:20, *"Satan meant it for evil, but God turned it around for good."*

One of the items we found while junking was a Kerosene heater, which turned out to be a disaster! Not having any experience with a Kerosene heater, I turned it down too much one evening. We awoke with the heater puffing, flames shooting high, and black soot landing everywhere. That heater sounded like a steam engine locomotive.

Our two children woke with their faces totally black and the whites of their eyes in sharp contrast to everything else around them. Fortunately, by then, we had lots of German whitewash wall paint and a washing machine. We spent the rest of the night cleaning up. We praised and thanked the Lord that the fire was contained in the heater. God supernaturally protected us.

A LIGHT IN A DARK PLACE

Matthew 5:16, *"Let your light so shine before men that men may see your good deeds and glorify your Father in Heaven."*

The location for our coffeehouse was in a rough part of Mannheim. The area had many bars and prostitutes (which were legal in Germany). There were Greeks, Turks, and people of other nationalities living there.

As we worked on the coffee shop every day, God would bring us G.I.'s and young German people to be saved and delivered. Every day God supplied the need through these precious young people. When the rent was due, we had more than enough to supply all our needs. A local Army chaplain donated all kitchen items, plus an abundance of coffee, cream, cups, and a much-needed dishwasher.

Some American teenagers got marvelously saved and turned their high school upside down for Christ. Every night ten to fifteen precious German and American young people were getting saved and baptized in the Holy Spirit. Sheryl was invited to host a Bible Study at the local high school cafeteria once a week. It was a wonderful time of spiritual harvest.

REFLECTIONS:

God often places people in our path to provide what is needed to accomplish His purposes through us. Although He owns the cattle on a thousand hills, He needs willing souls to be His hands and feet through giving.

When have you made yourself available to provide what someone else needed to accomplish God's will? Ask the Lord to show you opportunities, this day, where you might share a word of encouragement or invest in someone through your time and gifts.

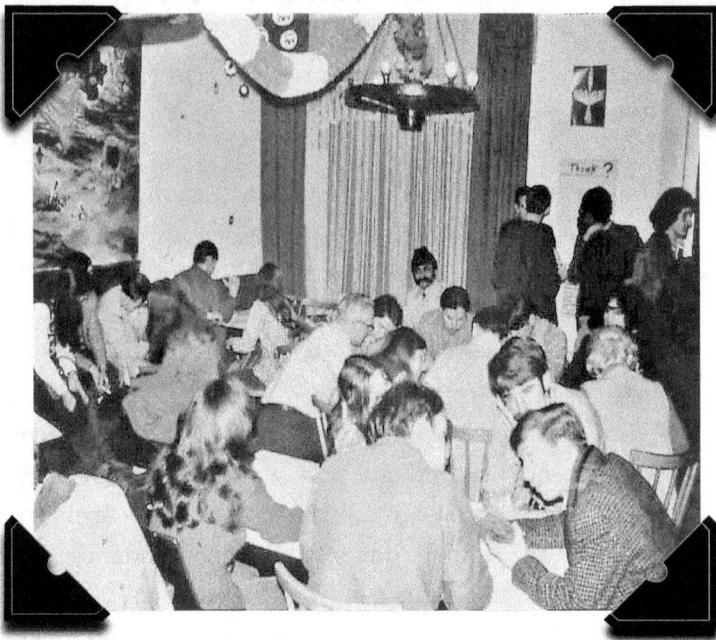

Mannheim Coffee House

CHAPTER 8

OTIS HOLMAN'S CONVERSION

*There will be more joy in Heaven over one
sinner who repents than over ninety-nine
righteous men who need no repentance*

Luke 15:7

ONE OF OUR EARLY CONVERTS was Otis Holman, an army
sergeant. During a church service altar call, I turned around
and asked Otis if he would like to come to the altar with me.
He replied, "I sure would." God saved him and delivered him
from smoking and alcohol.

Otis was my right-hand man in the early stages of building
our coffeehouse and had contacts for everything we needed.
Upon his discharge from the military, Otis went to
Southeastern Assemblies of God Bible School and into the
ministry. We visited him for the first time in 2015 in his
home in Florida and had a glorious prayer meeting and time
of recounting the blessings of God in those early days in
Germany.

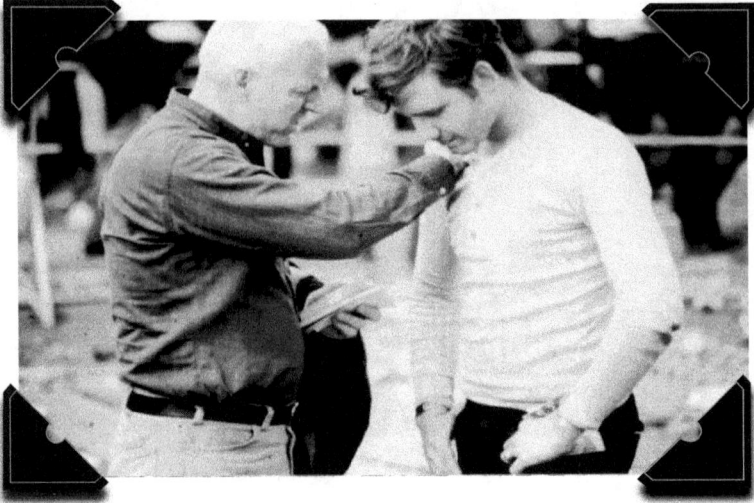

Otis Holman Praying for Young Soldier

A DESPERATE NEED FOR A HOME FOR JOACHIM

James 1:27, *"True religion is to visit the fatherless and widows in their affliction."*

One day, a couple of German social workers appeared at our coffeehouse with a fourteen-year-old boy named Joachim. The social workers said his father had chased his mother out of a third-story window to her death. They asked if we would temporarily take him in. We made the personal sacrifice and took him in, temporarily moving Ricky out of his bedroom.

Our willingness to take him in on short notice amazed the social workers, who arranged for the German television to interview us at the coffeehouse on site. The word got out that God was doing wonderful things at JA4A Mannheim, Germany. We were also interviewed by CBS United States television. Later, we were on the 700 Club in America with Pat Robertson.

One day, a fifteen-year-old German girl appeared at our door and asked us, "Is this where I can get saved?"

We had written in bold letters on one of our large plate glass windows: JESUS LOVES YOU. One night as we were cleaning up at about 2 a.m., a disheveled prostitute slowly walked by, and we overheard her say as she read the sign, "At least someone loves me."

APPLYING FOR A GERMAN VISA

Proverbs 28:1, *"The righteous are as bold as a lion."*

Early on at Mannheim, I applied for a visa that would enable us to stay in Germany. The man behind the desk said we must post money in escrow or return immediately since we had no visible means of support and no return ticket.

The Holy Spirit moved on me to boldly tell him about young people getting saved and delivered from drugs. Unintentionally, but rather emphatically, I found myself thumping his desk with my fist as I told him Germany should be paying for us and the good work we were doing for the young German people. He quickly changed his mind and stamped our passports.

I thought later he could just as quickly have rejected my request but thank God he changed his mind. Later, we were granted our nonprofit status. We were able to sign for scores of young people for visas, so they could come on staff and work with us in our coffeehouse. God's favor was on us and made it all so very easy for several years to come.

GOSPEL TRACTS

Psalm 68:11, *"The Lord gave the Word, great was the company of those that published it."*

We needed a lot of tracts for our street ministry. These were very expensive to buy and what was available was not always ideal for our ministry. Then the "Chick Tracks" came out. It was a brand-new approach written in several languages. They were printed at the Youth with A Mission (YWAM) castle in southern Germany.

We put the new wine in the old cellar.

To initially get them known, they gave us several pallets of tracts, which we stored in the wine cellar of our Bensheim facility. We would jokingly say, "We put the new wine in the old cellar."

T. L. Osborne closed his facility in England and sent us an eighteen-wheeler full of tracts, books, and other materials. We slid them down the ramp to the cellar the same way the wine barrels rolled down. God over answered our prayers as stated in Ephesians 3:20, *"More than we could ask or even think."* And we were able to bless other ministries.

GOD TAKES CARE OF AN ORPHAN

Psalm 27:10, *"If my father and my mother forsake me, then the Lord will take me in."*

Our G.I.s would regularly hand out tracts on the Strassenbahn, the streetcar, on the way to the coffeehouse and back to the base. They gave a tract to a young German teenager named Rudy, who came to our coffeehouse and got gloriously saved. He kept coming to receive teaching, prayer and was baptized in the Holy Spirit. His mother was a prostitute, and he was living in an orphanage. He was apprenticing at a furniture store. One day, he told us he could no longer work there because his boss required him to lie about the merchandise.

Rudy came to live with us at Bensheim. He contacted his mother, and she promised to visit him. He was nineteen then and so very excited about the visit. He waited all day at the window, but she never showed up. We were so brokenhearted along with him.

Shortly after that, we sponsored him to attend Christ for the Nations Bible School in Dallas, Texas. On a funny side note: He told us that you could take one whole loaf of American bread at school, and it would make up one slice of good German bread. Ha! Rudy came back to Germany to be a full-time pastor.

REFLECTIONS:

The Bible gives explicit instruction for the care of widows and orphans. God cares very deeply for them and commands *us* to protect and care for them, too. But we shouldn't care for widows or orphans simply because the Lord commands. There is a rich blessing in serving others.

Part of the responsibility we have as Christian families is to show the love of Christ and to heal broken hearts by opening up our homes to others. It brought great joy to our family to host both Joachim and Rudy. During their time with our family, God allowed us to sow seeds of greatness into them.

Have you ever considered the mission and ministry opportunities within your own home?

CHAPTER 9

GERMAN LUTHERAN PASTOR WOLFGANG WERNER

These signs will accompany those who believe; they will speak with new tongues.

Mark 16:17

A LUTHERAN PASTOR, Wolfgang Werner, had seen so many of his young people gloriously saved and filled with the Holy Spirit and become excited about Jesus. He came to our coffeehouse and told me this story. He said, "I was sitting on my back porch looking through a blue haze of cigarette smoke when the thought occurred to me, 'why don't I go down to that coffeehouse and have them pray for me?'" He came to the Mannheim Coffeehouse and ordered me to pray for him.

I prayed in English and then in my prayer language. To my amazement, he said I was speaking in Hebrew and quoting a Psalm. He was at that very moment delivered from smoking and his empty religion. Later, he received the baptism in the Holy Spirit as he rolled on the floor in total contradiction of his usual proper demeanor.

Pastor Werner was instrumental in bringing many ministers and Catholic nuns to the coffeehouse to receive a charismatic blessing. He took me to the Lutheran and Catholic seminaries to talk about the baptism in the Holy Spirit.

On one occasion, as Ricky witnessed to a very stately German gentleman, he said, "My father is Elijah, and I am Elisha." Out of the mouth of babes!

CROWDED COFFEEHOUSE AND IN NEED OF ADDITIONAL ROOMS

Isaiah 54:2, *"Enlarge the place of your tent and let them stretch out the curtains of your habitations and spare not."*

Very quickly, the coffeehouse was crowded with new converts. We had two bedrooms, a small kitchen, and a living room in the back of the coffeehouse. These rooms were used for prayer rooms and one where the young people played and sang.

The coffeehouse was full nightly, where young people were being witnessed to. We had to put our Ricky and Sharla to bed in the living room to sleep. We were crowded out. I talked to Herr Dietrich, the owner of the three-story building, and asked him for the next available apartment. He assured me that wouldn't happen because tenants handed their apartments to their relatives.

To our amazement, he showed up a couple of days later, saying an apartment was being vacated just above our coffeehouse. He had witnessed many miracles of salvation and deliverance, and he gave us the apartment at a bargain price. At Sheryl's insistence, since she wanted a bathtub for our children. I put in a new bathtub, a small sink, and a new stool—even though the room was way too small.

Sheryl and I must have been a comical sight carrying the bathtub through the street from the Bauhouse, like Home Depot. We had the only bathtub in the whole building. Our neighbors would come and ring the doorbell saying, "Ich will deine Badewanna sehen," which means, "I want to see your new bathtub."

I also put in a new kitchen with a corner bench. We put in new, little square carpeting and transformed it into a lovely apartment.

GOD DIRECTING US TO OPEN A HEIDELBERG COFFEEHOUSE

Matthew 28:19, *"Go and make disciples of all nations, baptizing them in the name of the Father, and of the Son and of the Holy Spirit."*

In just a few months, we were inundated with "on fire" young people who were leading others to Christ and discipling their peers. At that juncture, God laid it on our hearts to open a coffeehouse in Heidelberg, about ten miles from Mannheim.

As we prayed about this, God gave Sheryl a vision of ripe golden grain piling up on the cobblestone streets of old Heidelberg. This was a confirmation; the timing was right for a harvest of souls. After Sheryl and I prayed, I went to Heidelberg, and God directed me to the closed-up Salvation Army facility.

I rang the doorbell there and met Captain Lamonski. She was so excited and graciously allowed us to use the facility; we only had to pay for the utilities. It had a kitchen and a large room for church services, complete with chairs. We used the same large meeting room for the coffeehouse during the week. The coffeehouse was ideally located across from the main Heidelberg University building and near the renowned Holy Ghost Church, where many young people sat on the steps and did their drugs.

The altar call response was overwhelming. God's favor was with us.

In our opening service, the place was packed with people standing all around the walls, so we opened the windows to the courtyard, where there was standing room only. The altar call response was overwhelming. God's favor was with us.

OUR SON RICKY BAPTIZED IN THE HOLY SPIRIT

Acts 2:39, *"The promise is to you and your children and to all who are far away."*

On the way home from this powerful service, riding in our little VW hatchback, we were ecstatic at what God had done. As we praised and thanked God for His favor, we heard a strange language coming from the back seat. Our Ricky, age five, had received the mighty baptism in the Holy Spirit with no coaching and no one praying for him.

When we got home, I carried him into our apartment; he was still speaking in tongues for a long time until he fell asleep. Never underestimate a child's receptivity to the Holy Spirit.

Heidelberg Coffee House

A Gathering at Heidelberg Coffee House

We did street marches and meetings each Saturday at the Stadt Halle (town hall) in Heidelberg. For one of our services,

Willard Cantelon preached to hundreds of young people excited to hear the Gospel. Immediately, we needed additional help for the new coffeehouse ministry.

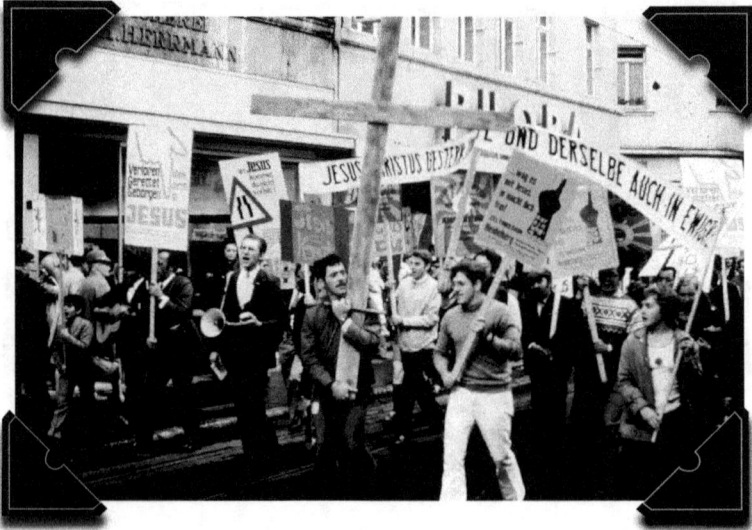

Our Street Marches Were Very Effective

NEEDED WORKERS FOR THE HEIDELBERG COFFEE HOUSE

Matthew 9:38, *"Pray to the Lord of the harvest that he will send out laborers into the harvest field."*

God miraculously sent a wonderful family to lead the Heidelberg coffeehouse for a year. Dr. Joe Nicolson, head of the music department of the Assembly of God Evangel College in Springfield, Mo., and his family were visiting us from Brussels when God spoke to them about coming for a year to assist.

I hastily put together a tiny apartment for them in the vacant three-hundred-year-old cloister behind the Salvation Army facility. I had to build a bathroom, complete with a shower and a kitchen. Although Dr. Joe, JoEllen, and their three children lived in primitive and cramped quarters, they had great enthusiasm and appreciation.

They ministered nightly to our G.I.s and the young German people. Only eternity will tell the magnitude of their sacrifice, love, and ministry. They were genuinely dedicated servants who brought many to a saving knowledge of Christ through their love and ministry.

Street March Every Saturday

REFLECTIONS:

Before Jesus ascended to Heaven, he told the disciples the Holy Spirit would come down upon them with power. And at Pentecost, they received the Holy Spirit with tongues of fire. The ministry of each disciple was never the same again!

Today every believer is indwelt by the Holy Spirit, who brings that same wisdom and power witnessed at Pentecost. Just as the disciples of Jesus' day, we have ministry opportunities through the Holy Spirit's leading. Are you taking advantage of this awe-inspiring truth?

Dr. Joe Nicholson

JoEllen Nicholson in Coffee House

CHAPTER 10

GOD'S AWESOME PROVISION

*I have given you every place that the sole of
your foot shall tread.*

Joshua 1:3

DRUGS WERE SO VERY RAMPANT on the Army bases. The drug situation was so bad they removed all the doors in the barracks rooms. Our G.I.s were desperate to be in a spiritual atmosphere and would bring their sleeping bags and stay the entire weekend with us at the coffee shop.

We knew God was leading us to find a larger facility as we were bursting at the seams. After some compelling prayer meetings and fasting, Pastor Werner located a large facility at 100 Dermstader St, in Bensheim, Germany. Benshiem was located halfway between Heidelberg and Darmstadt, Germany. The incredible 1904 mansion had thirty-seven rooms, plus a three-story addition, which was built after WWII. It was built to house a girdle factory.

We would jokingly tell people *they* reformed the body, but *we* reform the soul. Upon the initial viewing, we did a Jericho march all over the whole facility and claimed it for God. Though we didn't have any money, the owners agreed to let us move in and begin revamping the premises for our purposes. After establishing a German nonprofit organization, we would sign the papers—which would take about three months.

Bensheim Road View

In the meantime, our priority was to convert the main factory into a chapel that would seat three hundred. We worked, broke up, and threw out heavy metal sewing and rivet machines. In that era, girdles were made from metal staves that women wore in their bras and girdle and waist corsets. We used the wood shelving from the basement to build a platform in the beautiful chapel. It had large windows on both sides. But we had no money to carpet it.

The Rear-View at Bensheim

TESTIMONIES OF HEALING AND PROVISION

James 5:15, *"And the prayer of faith shall save the sick and the Lord will raise him up."*

Bill Norton was sent to us by Teen Challenge. Bill had been a teenager living with his parents in Holland and was hopelessly hooked on drugs. One day, he was wandering in Amsterdam traffic in a drug stupor. A driver rescued him from almost certain death. He ended up in a hospital where the doctors told his mother he would either not make it or be a vegetable.

His mother, being a Christian and a praying woman, called the Assemblies of God Missionary Howard Folt to the hospital. Howard laid hands on Bill, and a tremendous spiritual battle ensued. Bill came out of the coma and soon went to Teen Challenge in Holland. Shortly after that, he came to work with us at Bensheim.

Today, Bill Norton is an international evangelist of great anointing and power to this day. He experiences signs and wonders wherever he ministers.

Sheryl's mom and dad, Rev. and Mrs. Paul Sturgeon, came to help us for two years, along with Sheryl's two sisters, Sherry and Shauna. Sheryl's parents would spend hours with Bill, telling him of all the miracles they had witnessed.

For example, Sheryl's father was sent home to die from the Army. His skull was cracked in seven directions leaving him paralyzed on his right side, which was 1/3 smaller than the left side.

Just like you would blow up a balloon, God instantly healed me.

At the Oklahoma District Council, attended by three-thousand ministers and wives, Dr. Wallace Bragg asked attendees if they believed God could heal Paul Sturgeon. The ministers and wives began to pray, and my father-in-law said, "Just like you would blow up a balloon, God instantly healed me."

He went back to the Army doctors, and they could not believe he was the same Paul Sturgeon. The head doctor said, "I guess the big boy has to come down every once in a while, to show He is still up there.

Many other mighty miracles were shared with Bill Norton. Throughout the years, we have had Bill minister in our churches. He is a modern-day Book of Acts preacher and a great friend.

One day at just the right time, two men came by asking what we were doing with the facility. We explained it would be Christ for Europe and Teen Challenge and would serve all nationalities and the American soldiers. The two men invited Bill and me to their Christian convention nearby. Bill gave a powerful personal testimony, and I shared from the Word and gave facts about our ministry.

The leader spontaneously emptied one of the breadbaskets at his table and passed it around for an offering. We came away with more than enough for a brand-new red carpet for our three-hundred-seat chapel. Psalm 34:10, *"They who seek the Lord shall not be in want of any good thing."*

Sheryl's Parents, Paul & Maxine Sturgeon

We were on a roll. Things were coming together, and we began moving some of our equipment to the new facility. It was a blessing to obtain a surplus of Army bunks for one dollar each. Sheryl and I were able to pick and choose the best; most were barely used. We could sleep ninety male soldiers and had twenty bunk beds for female soldiers.

We were also blessed to get fantastic stainless-steel kitchen items for ten cents a pound from the Army surplus depot. Our kitchen had military stainless-steel appliances, including a commercial dishwasher, sink, and cabinets. On the weekend, we cooked and served an American meal for all our guests for free. There was a large serving area that the girdle factory had used for their employees. God knew years before that we would need such an excellent facility!

On each floor, there were seven sinks and seven toilets. I replaced one of the toilet stalls on each floor with a shower. We converted the third floor into an office and guest meeting room, staff rooms, and a small apartment for Sheryl's parents.

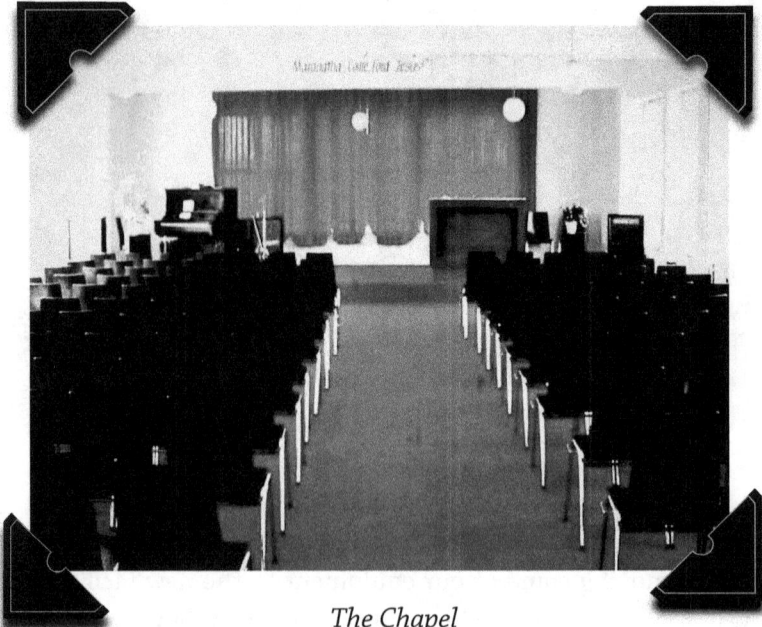

The Chapel

In the new section on the third floor, we had dormitory space for our G.Is and a library. Sheryl's mom was a county librarian in Texas and set up a first-class library for our guests. We had a conference room that seated forty, and on

Saturday morning, a Bible Study room. Best of all, we had a large prayer room with an altar in the middle. Every Tuesday was our fast and prayer day, where God would meet with us and give Divine guidance for our ministry and coffeehouses.

The Cafeteria at Bensheim

The Christ for Europe Staff

Bible Study

Chapel Service at Bensheim

Chapel services were well attended. They usually consisted of prayer, songs of worship, and Bible teaching. There are now several pastors and church leaders and numerous ministry volunteers active in ministry today that once attended these services. These chapel services were a blessing and encouragement to everyone—the leaders and the students— as we worshipped and studied God's Word together.

REFLECTIONS:

Can you imagine starting off on a journey to somewhere that you've never been without a map or explicit directions? It would be nearly impossible to reach our destination without some guidance or instruction.

The Holy Spirit is our spiritual GPS. We simply need to follow, and He will open doors that no man can shut. How often do we make life complicated by not listening to the Lord and not choosing to follow Him? Often, we miss out on God's provision by ignoring His lead. Pray for the Lord to direct your steps and guide you along His path.

CHAPTER 11

MEETING WITH THE GERMAN CITY COUNCIL

He has put a new song in my mouth, even praise to our God. Many will see it and fear and will trust in the Lord.

Psalm 40:3

IN MY MEETING WITH THE GERMAN CITY COUNCIL, I presented our case in my best, yet not so good, German. I knew our workers were praying fervent, heartfelt prayers, making tremendous power available, which is dynamic in its workers (James 5:16 AMP). Suddenly, I felt a burst of power and began to talk about young people who were being delivered from drugs and finding new life in Jesus!

The council members leaned forward to hear what I was sharing and unanimously approved our nonprofit religious application at the end of the meeting. God continued to supply our daily needs. Sometimes our finances came from the U.S. and sometimes from the Germans, but mainly from the G.I.s we were ministering to.

DOWN PAYMENT MONEY NEEDED

Luke 13:7, *"For with God, nothing will be impossible."*

Then all of a sudden, it seemed the day of reckoning was upon us. Our nonprofit had been approved, which spared us the taxes. We were notified by the owners on Friday that we were to appear on Monday with the down payment and to sign the closing papers. We prayed earnest prayers and put the word out to the helpers we had ministered to.

A Catholic church donated about $1000; we had previously made presentations in their orphanage about God's power to deliver from drug addiction. We received a donation from the German Lutheran churches and individuals because they had experienced God's healing and delivering power in some area of their lives. By far, the bulk of donations came from our G.I.s. Scores had been saved, delivered from drug addictions, and were now living a new life in Christ.

One of those precious young people brought us $2,000 in twenty-dollar bills. He said, "I was saving this to buy a new car upon my discharge. But I got saved here and delivered from drugs and have a new life. I want the ministry to continue for others."

There were countless such stories from young people who rallied to the challenge. This continued all day Saturday and in our Sunday afternoon service while in our brand-new carpeted chapel, as young people gave to the ministry.

On Sunday night, after the coffeehouse activities, knowing we had to pay the down payment the next day, we started counting. We counted German money and other European monies and set it aside. Most of the G.I.s had paid in $20 bills.

We made short stacks of $100 each on our large table. Once finished, we counted and came up short of the $30,000 needed. The Lord spoke to me, "Count it again."

So, we did, and every stack contained $120! We were awestruck and ecstatic at the same time. We made extra $100 stacks, and still, we were short. The Lord said, "Count it again."

We did, and the same thing happened. Every stack had $120. We were still short but had the reassurance God would supply. God supernaturally had multiplied the money!

On Monday, as we were preparing to go to the meeting, Bruce Bussel, a young Air Force Captain, came rushing up to our driveway. He said he had withdrawn his donation as soon as the bank opened and had driven his BMW from Frankfurt as fast as possible (*German autobahns at that time had no speed limit*). He gave us a $3,000 donation and had arrived just before we left for our meeting. We put the monies in a blue metal box and presented them at the meeting. It was perfect! Best of all, we signed the purchase contract.

> *God supernaturally had multiplied the money!*

Three months later, our first installment was due the following day, but we did not have the money. It was a Tuesday, and I instituted a prayer and fast day for Sheryl, the staff, and myself. We had several young people who were volunteers and "on fire" for God. They had either been saved in our ministry or had come from the States to help us and Elsie, a precious German lady, who felt led to minister with us.

We prayed all day, and the Lord spoke to me to read the contract. I discovered the payment was not due until a month later! By that time, we had the money for the payment. From that time on, every Tuesday was a staff prayer and fast day.

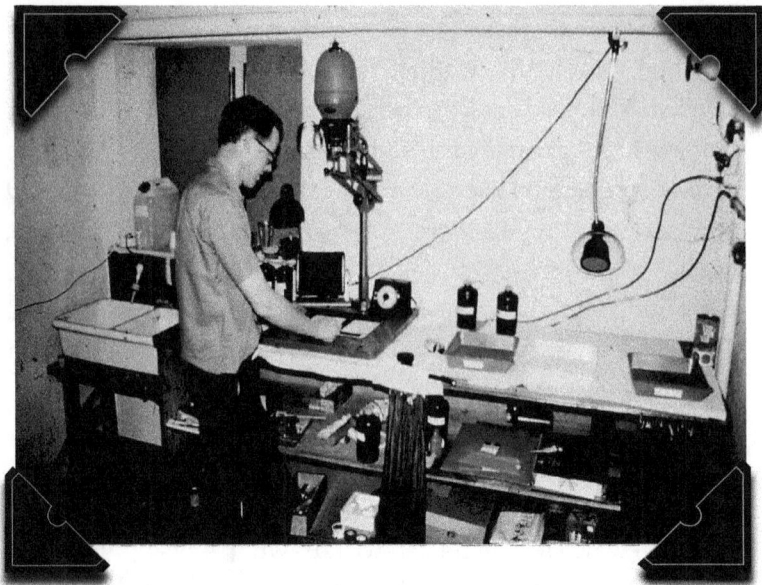

Bruce Bussel in his photo lab

OUR FURNACE QUIT

Isaiah 65:24, *"Before they call, I will answer, and while they are yet speaking, I will hear."*

One day, our furnace quit. Upon examination, the furnace man said he would order the main part if I could guarantee I would pay him the $450 when they delivered. We did not have the money, but I assured him we would pay the total amount upon delivery. On the very day, a check arrived from Mom and Pop Dankert's Church in the states for exactly $450.

Dave Dankert Gloriously Saved

2 Corinthians 5:17, *"Therefore if any man is in Christ, he is a new creature. Old things have passed away. Look, all things have become new."*

Mom and Dad Dankert's son, Dave, had gotten saved in our coffeehouse ministry. God had radically turned his life around, and Dave was undoubtedly a "new person in Christ." The old things had passed away, and behold, all things had become new.

When his Mom and Dad came to visit him in Germany, they were so amazed at the change in their son they spent most of their vacation time in our coffeehouse working with our young people. Upon getting ready to leave, they asked if they could come back and work with us for a year. Of course, we said, "Yes." We were always in need of helpers, especially those who could pay their own way.

Mr. Dankert was an executive with IBM and asked for a one-year leave of absence. At first, he was denied. He told them, "God called us to help in Germany. If you do not give me a year of absence, I'll go anyway."

His boss granted his request. As they affectionately became known by our G.I.s, "Mom and Pop" Dankert ran the third coffeehouse on an Army Base in Darmstadt, where their son Dave was stationed.

This coffeehouse named *Crossroads* was arranged for us by the then Commanding General of the Darmstadt base. The General wanted a place for his troops to go for spiritual and social input. He provided a room right off the mess hall that was formerly used for the officers to dine. It was a lovely room, perfect for a coffeehouse.

Scores of G.I.s were saved and filled with the Holy Spirit in the Darmstadt coffeehouse. Mom and Pop Dankert were anointed, loving, and dedicated to the work and ministry of the coffeehouse.

One young man, Phil Ponessa, was saved in the front seat of Dave Dankert's little Fiat car after visiting the coffeehouse. I remember him telling me he struggled to kneel in that cramped space because he thought he had to kneel to pray. Since his discharge, Phil has served the Lord in ministry in his hometown for the last thirty-seven years.

Phil Ponessa being baptized
while Bill Norton & Pastor Boettiger look on

Mom and Pop Dankert at the Crossroads Coffee Shop

REFLECTIONS:

The circumstances in our life often come with deadlines and due dates. We live in Chronos (chronological) time which runs on minutes, hours, and days. But God's timing is eternal. He is never in a hurry, and He's never late. He's always on time!

Recall a situation in your life when the Lord was working behind the scenes, putting together just what you needed to meet a deadline. Did it seem like you weren't going to meet your obligation or due date? But did the Lord show up at just the right moment to meet your need? Thank Him now for His always-perfect timing.

CHAPTER 12

BENSHEIM 100 DARMSTADER ST. REHABILITATION MINISTRY

A gentle word, a kind look, and a good-natured smile can work wonders and accomplish miracles.

William Hazlitt

THE CENTER WAS BECOMING more and more active. We had added a rehabilitation ministry, which consisted mainly of Jesus in the morning, the Father at noon, and the Holy Spirit in the evening! We discovered that huge, intense prayer and Bible reading doses would deliver from sin and its addictions when applied to a sincere heart. Our staff was doing just that.

Colonel Curry, a Spirit-filled Army Colonel who would soon become the youngest General in the U.S. Army, would bring us young men who were addicts or alcoholics, in a last-ditch effort for a cure, just before a medical discharge from the military. Marvin Armbruster was one of them. Marvin absented himself from our center. He was AWOL as he hid in the woods. Our precious dedicated staff lovingly ministered to him in the woods and brought him back to the center. Marvin became gloriously saved and delivered and flushed his stash down the toilet. 2 Timothy 2:2 tells us that the spiritual truths we have been taught are to be introduced to others.

BENSHEIM CENTER OF OPERATIOn

1 Corinthians 3:9, *"For we are laborers together with God."*

Bensheim was our center of operations. From there, we manned the coffeehouse, held meetings, and conducted all our business. We never knew how many people would spend the weekend with us. This uncertainty would be compounded by the scores of G.I.s who drove in to participate.

We supported the local churches and military chapels on Sunday mornings. On Sunday afternoon, we had our own service in our 300-seat chapel. Our Son-Light band would lead the worship.

Our belief was to conduct a three-part service: First, an excellent ministry of music, then a powerfully anointed preaching, and finally, an altar invitation and an opportunity to respond to God on a very personal level. It was so thrilling to see young people from every walk of life worshipping God with their whole hearts.

Most of the participants had no religious background. Those who needed Friday night accommodations could come home with them to Bensheim for further ministry. Every Saturday, we would have ninety men and about twenty women.

There was a full schedule of ministry on Saturday. It began with breakfast for all. Then at ten, singing was led by our Son-Light band in the conference room, followed by an excellent Bible Study. There was a lot of praise and rejoicing as new converts received the Holy Spirit. We also had seasonal recreation on Saturday afternoons. After the evening meal, we all headed to different coffeehouses.

The Son-Light Band

Miracles of Provision

Galatians 6:9, *"Let us not grow weary in doing well, for, in due season, we shall reap if we do not give up."*

On those ministry weekends, we experienced many miracles of God's provision. One day, a German farmer brought in four hundred pounds of potatoes. We had fun discovering all the ways to fix potatoes. We did not charge for the meals; everyone who came to the center was fed at no charge. And God would multiply the food. Our wonderful cooks prayed their way through many food crises!

One young sixteen-year-old was brought to us by her pastor and parents. She was their only child and on drugs. However, she received Christ and was set free. Months later, the pastor gave us a significant check to buy groceries for our center.

A Motorcycle Gang Visits our Center

Romans 8:28, *"We know all things work together for good to those who love God, to those who are called according to His purpose."*

One evening, after all the staff had gone to their respective coffeehouses, I remained in our garage at the back of our center to work on one of our VW buses that needed repair. We had built a grease pit in one of the garages to maintain our worn-out VW vans, so they could be fixed. I loved working on the vans and taught some of our G.I.s how to repair engines.

Sheryl was on the third floor in our apartment with Ricky, Sharla, and Liana. In response to the doorbell, she pushed the button which allowed the door to open, assuming it was me.

A motorcycle gang quickly entered. We found out later they were bent on destroying our place.

Sheryl looked downstairs to the open entry from the third floor and saw the gang coming up. She quickly put the kids in the bathroom and locked the door, and the apartment door, then ran down to meet them.

The Holy Spirit had her divert them with her kindness, and she welcomed them to the center. In her best German, she said, "Great to see you, let me make you some American popcorn and cold drinks."

She directed them to the large prayer room and gave them American treats. It totally surprised them! The Darmstadt Coffee House crew unexpectedly came home early and joined Sheryl in ministering the Gospel to them. The motorcycle gang was in shock. The Holy Spirit had taken charge of the situation!

Totally oblivious to what was happening, I came in and saw our team praying with several of these gang members. Others were getting very nervous about the whole situation. God's mission was accomplished, and theirs went flat. God thwarted their plans with kindness and popcorn! This was a treat because Germans did not eat popcorn in the 1970s.

A year later, Mom and Pop Dankert visited Amsterdam, Holland. They heard a street preacher on the foundation at the square. A crowd of young people was intently listening to him preach the Word of God. Mom and Pop drew closer to

He had been so drastically changed by the power of God...

listen to the young preacher as he bolted off the foundation used for his platform. He began hugging them, and he asked if they remembered him. They did not recognize this man who was clean-shaven and dressed so respectfully.

Turns out, he was the head of the motorcycle gang that had come to destroy our center in Bensheim! He had been so drastically changed by the power of God that he wanted to share a life of purpose and direction with others. It was Mom and Pop's team from Darmstadt that had come home early that fateful day to minister to that gang.

FATHER STOCK, A CATHOLIC PRIEST FROM LUDWIGSHAFEN

John 3:3, *"Truly, truly I say to you unless a man is born again, he cannot see the kingdom of God.*

A Catholic priest named Father Stock came from his parish in Ludwigshafen, a city adjacent to Mannheim. He told us he was born again in Hamburg when some Jesus people witnessed to him. He said that at first, he was offended because he was wearing his priest's clothing. They sidestepped religion and asked him about a personal relationship with Christ. Under conviction of the Holy Spirit, he knelt on the cobblestone sidewalk and accepted Christ. He was so excited when he talked to us and said, "Now I have something to say and give that I did not have before."

Father Stock came weekly and ultimately received the Holy Spirit with the evidence of speaking in a Heavenly language. He invited our Son-Light band to minister in music, and I was asked to preach to a thousand parishioners at his church in Ludwigshafen on a Saturday evening. His overseer, Father Schmitt, from the whole region of Catholic Churches and the Catholic retreats for young people, came to the meeting. I told Father Stock I didn't want to get him in trouble. But at the end of the service (mass), Father Schmitt approached me and said, "I want what you have!" and I planned for him to come to our center in Bensheim on Monday morning.

Father Stock at Bensheim

ECUMENICAL MEETING IN THE HOLY SPIRIT

Acts 1:8, *"You shall receive power when the Holy Spirit comes upon you."*

I began teaching Father Stock about Baptism in the Holy Spirit. After spending a couple of hours in scripture, a local Lutheran pastor, Pastor Moen, joined us. Pastor Moen had experienced a very rough Sunday and needed encouragement. His hair was messed up, and his demeanor was downcast.

He told Sheryl, "I must see your husband."

Sheryl directed him to where I was ministering to Father Schmitt. The three of us continued to study the Word on the Holy Spirit, and then we went to prayer. Both men were hungry for all God had for them, and they joyfully received it.

It was about four in the afternoon, and Sheryl decided to bring some tea and cakes, a German tradition, to the room where we were. She opened the door to find that Father Moen was under the coffee table, earnestly praying in the Holy Spirit. Father Schmitt was sitting up against the wall with hands raised, praising God in tongues. I, true to my Pentecostal upbringing, was dancing around ecstatically praising God in tongues.

Sheryl was so amazed as she joined us in prayer and praise. Later, she said, "This was truly an ecumenical meeting." Praise God! When we remove our man-made barriers and go straight to the Word of God, He does beautiful things.

REFLECTIONS:

The Bible instructs us to live as a "light on a hill"—reflecting something others would be drawn to and want for themselves. In a world of hate and judgment, the True Light is comforting, appealing, and illuminating. It comes through Jesus and directs us.

Do you have that light in your heart? Or do you keep it hidden? Ask the Lord to show you how to live in such a way that people want what you have—the light of the Holy Spirit living in and through you.

CHAPTER 13

EXCITING TIMES OF MINISTRY

Behold, I will do a new thing.

Isaiah 43:19

ONE DAY, Father Stock, previously mentioned, brought a teenage girl to us for prayer and possible admission into our rehabilitation program. She had been in many programs, all to no avail. Her parents entrusted Father Stock to take care of her, knowing the girl was a very rebellious young lady who had run away several times.

As we were talking, she bolted out the door and down the street. Father Stock, who was in priestly garb, followed in full pursuit. He caught up with her and somehow hooked her arm around a stop sign post as she tried to cut him with a small pocketknife.

All ended well; we prayed with her and her parents. We had some belly laughs as we reminisced over what the passing motorists thought about that priest trying to corral that teenage girl while she was trying to stab him. He told me he never experienced adventure in ministry before he was saved and filled with the Holy Spirit. I think of Peter being catapulted out of a life of fishing into an exciting life of miracles, signs, and wonders.

OUR WONDERFUL BREAD TRUCK

Luke 6:38, *"Give, and it will be given you: Good measure, pressed down, shaken together and running over shall men give unto you."*

God provided us with a step van for our ministry. In a very interesting way, someone in the army motor pool fixed up the bread truck with a new motor, tires, and brakes and put it in top shape to ship back to America for a camper. But he found out customs would not allow him to send it to America.

One of our G.I.s snatched it up for one-hundred-fifty dollars at the surplus sale. We drove what we affectionally called "God's Bread Truck" and drove it for many years with practically no maintenance expense.

Our Son-Light band would use the bread truck on weekends to go to chapels and other places of ministry. One of these young G.I.s, John Buckarie, became, and still is, an Assembly of God missionary.

ROCK FESTIVAL IN SPEYER, GERMANY ON PENTECOST SUNDAY

II Timothy 1:7, *"For God has not given us the spirit of fear, but of power, and love and of self-control."*

Several Lutheran and Catholic ministers invited us to take part in a Pentecost Sunday meeting in Speyer. The Lutheran and Catholic ministers had made arrangements with the Rock Band Company to use an extensive valley area for a Rock Festival with the stipulation that they would allow a Pentecost Sunday morning service.

When Pentecost Sunday morning came, we loaded up our bread truck with two pallets of tracts and twenty-one young people and met the ministers at the local church in Speyer. They went on ahead of us, explained their mission to the guards, and were waved through the gate. They had their clergy clothes on, which validated them.

When we came at the end of the line, the guards, which were Hell's Angels complete with chains, brass knuckles, and large guard dogs, would not let us through the gate. The cost to enter was very high, and they thought we only wanted to come in without paying. We explained we had come to minister and had been invited to share on this particular Pentecost Sunday with our band and the young people. We tried to convince the guards—to no avail!

We tried to convince the guards—to no avail!

It seemed all was lost when the Holy Spirit prompted Sheryl and me to spontaneously jump out of the bread truck and started speaking loudly in tongues, laying hands on these formidable-looking gang members. They very quickly let us go through the gate. It was as in Luke 4:30 when Jesus passed through the hostile crowd to minister to the demon-possessed man.

As we passed through the gate, we were immediately confronted with a heartbreaking scene. The valley below contained about one-hundred thousand young people in tents and blankets, all stoned out of their minds. It had rained the night before; there was mud and squalor everywhere. There was also a cloud of marijuana smoke for as far as you could see.

We arrived at the elevated platform in time to see our minister friends dejected and leaving the scene, informing us that the management had reneged on their promise and would not let them have the Pentecost Sunday morning Service.

We sprinted up two flights of stairs, prepared for a spiritual battle. We informed the management that we were going to have a service as they had initially agreed upon. Still, they refused. So, we formed a circle of twenty-three "Holy Ghost" anointed people who all began to pray in a loud and boisterous tone. We rebuked the devil and called on the Holy Spirit to tear down the obstacles. We were to be the first on the program.

The leader saw we were not going away. At this, the leader said, "We will ask the crowd if they want to hear from the Jesus People."

After about five minutes of allowing the amp to warm up and while we were still in fervent prayer, he sarcastically asked the massive crowd if they wanted to hear from the "Jesus People." To his amazement, the crowd roared affirmatively. They wanted to hear from us!

Our young people provided music and offered beautiful testimonies about how they had found new life in Jesus and had been delivered from addiction. I shared a Pentecost message with power and anointing. My heart was so stirred by the sight of all those lost souls that needed Jesus. We dispersed among the crowd all that day to give out tracts, share testimonies, and pray for those precious young people. Our bread truck became a prayer and deliverance facility for scores of young people. All throughout the day, we handed out hundreds of copies of an influential tract called a "Chick tract."

Looking back on this experience, it was not us, but the boldness of the Holy Spirit through us, that made the difference. Jesus said we would be baptized in the Holy Spirit and with fire. The opposition was confronted with the Holy Spirit flame thrower and went down in defeat!

In the wake of this momentous day, we had many young people come to our coffeehouses. They told us they were at the Rock Fest in Speyer and had come to know Christ or came to find Christ at the coffeehouses.

Witnessing at Rock Fest

Prayer in The Bread Truck

THE WAY BIBLES

Isaiah 55:11 *"So shall my Word be that goes forth from my mouth, it shall not return to me void, but it shall accomplish that which I please, it shall prosper in the things for which I sent it."*

Someone in Washington decided that every service member should have the opportunity to have a "Way Bible." It was the green easy-to-read living Bible version. Thousands of these wonderful Bibles were shipped to chapels across Europe. The problem was that even though the chaplain had potentially thousands in his military parish, perhaps only a fraction would attend chapel services. The chaplains had no place to store them. We had the perfect wine cellar in Bensheim for the "New Wine of the Word of God."

About that time, Father Stock and Father Schmitt invited us to participate in their Catholic school retreat schedule. In Germany, religion is taught in public schools. The class included a three-day retreat during the school year. They would spend three days on their retreat, and then another group would replace their group on a revolving basis.

I thought it would be wonderful if we could give every student an easy reading English Bible. In response to our request, chaplains offered us thousands of Bibles, which we gave to the young German people. During the retreat, we ministered to them, and our dedicated staff provided excellent music and testimonies. The team ministered and sang the praises of God, ministered the Word, and prayed with these young Catholic people to receive Christ as their personal Lord and Savior.

What a joy it was to hand each of them their very own Bible. They expressed great joy as m ost of them had never owned their own Bible. Most of them could read English, and this would give them a greater incentive to study English. And now, the Word of God was becoming a lamp to their feet.

The Word of God did not return void but accomplished the purposes to which it was sent (as in Isaiah 55:11). We know this opportunity is still bearing fruit to this day. I can't wait to see many of those young people in Heaven.

REFLECTIONS:

Who would ever think that an old bread truck could be an instrument in ministry for two young missionaries? And yet, this step van served as a blessing for many, many years. It was actually fixed up for another purpose, but the Lord knew it would fit a better need. We are not alone, moving our way blindly through life. God cares about every detail, including our transportation needs! Perhaps you have days where you don't think God is concerned toward you, and you've hit a dead end.

Understand that God isn't too big or too busy to work on the details in your life. He absolutely cares about every little thing that happens. Recall a time when He showed Himself faithful in a need, even when you thought He might not care.

Ricky & Sharla with their Way Bibles

CHAPTER 14

A "JESUS PEOPLE" CHURCH IN THE SCHOOL

Go therefore and teach all nations.

Matthew 28:19

A TREMENDOUS OPPORTUNITY was opened to us by the local German school system to demonstrate how "Jesus People" have church in their German Religious classes. The "Jesus People" movement was big news in the seventies, and we jumped at the opportunity. In the course, we would demonstrate a "Jesus People" church service complete with easy English songs, music, testimonies, and God's Word on Salvation. An altar call was always given, and we got the privilege to pray with many and give The Way Bibles to every student.

What a privilege, joy, and tremendous ministry opportunity we were given to share the love of God. You should have seen the smiles, as the young people enjoyed the live, vibrant, and joyful way to have church. We showed them the joy of a living relationship with an up-to-date God. Our staff was turned on to Jesus!

MILITARY, "PROJECT TRANSITION"

1 Corinthians 16:9, *"For a great and effective door has opened to me, and there are many adversaries."*

Early on, one of our first converts, Sgt. Otis Holman, mentioned previously, was instrumental in getting us involved in "Project Transition." This was an Army-sponsored program, which basically assigned a G.I. to a civilian workplace for on-the-job training during the last six months of their enlistment. Sgt. Holman requested to be assigned to our ministry in Bensheim because he was going into the ministry after his discharge. Initially, they denied his request due to the separation of church and state.

Otis said, "If someone can get six months paid assignment to learn a trade, I can get the same on-the-job training for my chosen profession, the ministry."

After nearly thirty years in the Army, Otis was relentless. Finally, they assigned him to our ministry, which enabled him to receive full pay while working full time in our ministry. This was a tremendous breakthrough for us as it became the avenue for scores of G.I.s to help us in the ministry. Many of these fine young men and women had no idea what they would do when they were discharged.

As they spent full-time in our ministry, which included much prayer, Bible study, coffeehouse ministry, and ministry in our chapel services, many were ultimately called into full-time ministry. At one time, we had thirty-five of these precious young people in Bible Colleges in the United States.

Project Transition continued for several years and was a great blessing to our ministry and scores of G.I.'s

AN UNUSUAL STREET MINISTRY VAN

I Cor 9:22, *"I have become all things to all men that I might save some."*

One day an engine blew up in one of our dilapidated vans. That same day Mike Little, an Army officer, donated his VW van to us. Mike Little later became President and CEO of Christian Broadcasting Network in Virginia Beach, Virginia. The van was unusual because it had a full-length sunroof that could be slid back to create a large opening. We converted it into a street ministry van. Our band could stand on benches in the van and be almost full-body visible to sing & play gospel music. Our staff would come along, too, to pass out gospel tracts.

Our young people loved the excitement and adventure!

There were times when the crowd blocked the street, where the police would come and request that we quickly move to another location at a moment's notice. We would start all over again with a completely new crowd. We referred to this as "blitz evangelism," taking the name from Hitler's "blitzkrieg" war tactics. Our young people loved the excitement and adventure!

TROUBLE IN THE STOCKADE-MILITARY PRISON

Matthew 25:36, *"I was in prison, and you came to me."*

In the early seventies, there was a riot at the U.S. Military Stockade, a military prison at Coleman Barracks, near

Mannheim. Having heard about the positive changes in the lives of our G.I.s coming to Jesus, the leadership at the Stockade requested that we begin a ministry in the prison. I felt inspired to start with "The Cross & the Switchblade."

Teen Challenge Bus

At first, they rejected this request as they were fearful of the possible consequences of assembling all the prisoners in one location in the gymnasium. They gave us permission and placed stringent safeguards, including adding extra guards for this one-time occasion. The atmosphere was tense as I gave introductory remarks about the movie about Dave Wilkerson's ministry to drug addicts in New York. I had prearranged with the stockade commanding officer to ask those who wanted to make a decision for Christ to form in single file and make their way to the chapel. There would be guards manning various stations along the way up to the chapel.

After the film, I gave a short salvation message, prayed for the participants, and gave the altar call. At first, no one broke rank. Then under heavy conviction, a young man got up and headed to the chapel, followed by scores of his peers.

I followed these men to the chapel and was greeted with a beautiful sight. Their conviction was so heavy. Several of these men were in tears of repentance; we spent several hours leading these precious ones to Jesus—individually and collectively.

After such a tremendous change in the prison atmosphere, we were asked to hold meetings each Wednesday in the Chapel. Sheryl enjoyed playing the piano and watching these men in a full prison chapel sing with all their souls. It was so exciting to hear the testimonies of those saved and filled with the Holy Spirit. Quite often, we would hear them say, "I am glad I am here because this is where I met Jesus, and my life got turned around."

Our staff and members from the Assemblies group in Mannheim would come with us. One lady named Kathy would bake a cake, brownies, cookies, and we would serve them after the service—a fellowship time with the prisoners. The commanding officer told me shortly after we began the prison ministry that the whole atmosphere of the entire prison had changed, and he was very grateful. We were also asked to hold retreats for the prisoners, and so we brought in special music and speakers from the States to minister to the inmates.

When we came back to the States, Jerry Groom, an Assemblies of God missionary, took over this awesome Prison Ministry. When Jerry came back to the United States, he became Director of Chaplains at the Texas Department of Criminal Justice.

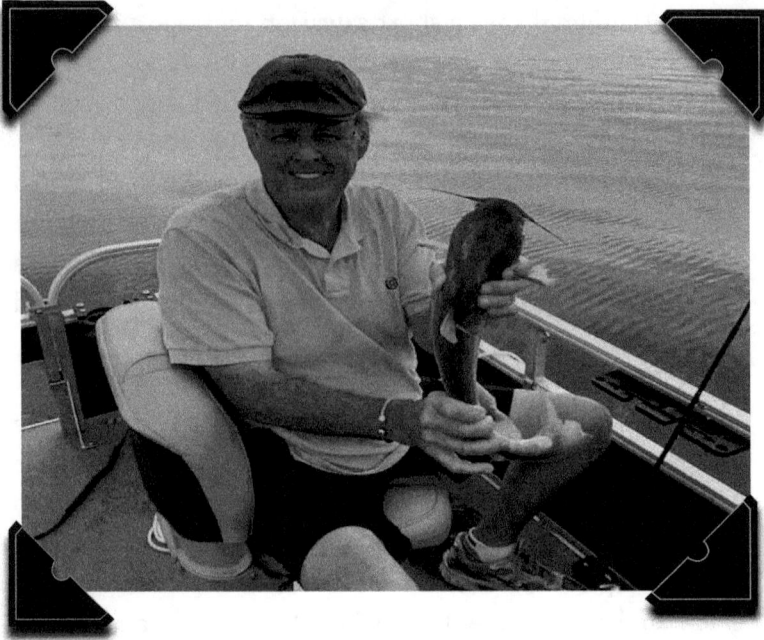

Jerry Groom 2018

A YOUNG MAN DELIVERED AND SET FREE. MATTHEW 10:8

In Mannheim, we were cleaning up one day about midnight with a German couple, Anita and Reiner Heppenstein. Reiner was a schoolteacher, and from time to time, he would come to minister the plan of salvation to our German guests. It was late, the front door to the coffeehouse was closed, and the rouladens (*shutters covering the big glass plate windows*) and door were down.

A young German man knocked on the entry door.; we were somewhat reluctant to let him in. We found out that Jochim was just released from prison and had nowhere to go. The Heppensteins were talking to him and ministering to him. When they spoke the name of "Jesus," he went crazy. He attacked them and tried to ram his head through the glass door.

We immediately went into spiritual warfare, unsuccessfully trying to hold him down while praying desperate prayers, pleading the Blood of Jesus over him. During this ensuing spiritual and physical battle, four of us held him down, Reiner and I on each arm and shoulder, Anita and Sheryl holding his legs. Jochim was struggling with power and might to get free, as the enemy wanted to destroy him and us as well.

At one point, Jochim kicked Sheryl in her belly with a very forceful blow. Sheryl was several months pregnant. By God's grace, mercy, and mighty power, Jochim was delivered and set free of demon possession. He became a new creature in Christ. This was the first encounter all of us had with someone that was demon-possessed.

A COMFORTING WORD FROM GOD

John 16:13, *"He will tell you things that are to come."*

Sheryl was so worried about the unborn baby in her womb and cried out to God that night. God gave her a vision of a two-year-old little girl on a red tricycle—perfect, with beautiful blue eyes. That was before an ultrasound machine was available.

Along with the vision came a peace that all was well with our baby. Several months later, our third child, Liana, was born. She was perfect, precious, and oh so loved. Liana is now forty-five and has two beautiful, charming girls of her own. She lives in Texas with her husband, Joe, who is a Delta pilot.

Our daughter Liana and her husband Joe

REFLECTIONS:

God values all human life, even those who are still in the womb. Psalm 139 says that He is personally involved in our formation and fully knows us before we are born.

Even with the ability to view a baby through ultrasound, there is no way that we can completely imagine what they will look like and what they will become. But God knows the end from the beginning. He sees every aspect of our lives before we have lived one moment in the world.

Have you ever considered that He knew you and had established your purpose, even before your birth? Thank Him at this moment for loving you from your conception to this day.

CHAPTER 15

PRAYER POWER OF A NEW BABE IN CHRIST

They brought their friend to Jesus.

Mark 2:3

It was customary for G.I.s to bring their friends to the coffeehouse to be saved. I remember Michael Spooner telling me, "I told him everything I know about Jesus, and he is still not saved, so please help me get my friend to know Jesus."

Perhaps above all the other stories, the one about Forest Stiltner stands out most. Michael, who brought him, said Forest had experienced an ego-death because of a drug overdose. He was going to be medevacked to the U.S. because they could do nothing to help him. Forest could barely talk and not very coherently.

We took him into the prayers room, laid hands on him, and desperately prayed. At the end of our lengthy prayer, Forest mumbled, "God, if you are up there, please help me."

When he awoke the following day, he was markedly better. All day long, he continued to improve. That evening back at the coffeehouse, he was a new person, totally healed by the power of God.

God, if you are up there, please help me.

Forest, a talented artist, illustrator, and musician, painted a beautiful mural for us on the coffeehouse wall. He was also part of our Son-Light band. He could play the banjo like nobody else.

The Son-Light Band would minister in chapels in the area, and Forest would give a powerful testimony of the love of God and salvation. His commanding officer saw the miracle in his life and said he was free to go and give his powerful testimony when needed. Forest is now married to a wonderful German lady and lives in Baltimore.

Mural by Forest Stiltner

THE MCCULLOUGH FAMILY TO HELP IN MINISTRY

Luke 10:2, *"The harvest truly is plentiful, but the laborers are few. Pray, therefore the Lord of the harvest to send forth laborers into His harvest."*

One day a military family, Sgt. Charles and Lou McCullough, came to visit us at Bensheim. Sheryl was ministering to their children, Gary and Raymond, on the front row in the Saturday morning Bible Study. During the powerful prayer time with our G.I.s and nationals, Raymond received the baptism of the Holy Spirit with the evidence of speaking in a heavenly language. What a glorious and blessed sight to behold as tears ran down his eight-year-old cheeks.

This sweet couple drove down every weekend from Kaiserslautern. Ricky now had two wonderful American kids to play ball with. Raymond and Ricky remained best of friends until God called Raymond home.

Lou would make desserts and special casseroles for our Sunday meals. Everyone loved Lou. Charles was a very studied man of the Bible and led our G.I.s to a more profound knowledge of God's Word.

Lou and Charles led our fourth coffeehouse in Viernheim. After retiring from the Army, they became Assemblies of God missionaries to our U.S. Servicemen in Kaiserslautern, where we also pastored for six years later on.

PIANO LESSONS MONEY FROM AN UNLIKELY SOURCE

Matthew 17:27, *Jesus said, "Take the first fish that comes up, open its mouth you will find a coin."*

We also hosted many parents of our G.I.s that came to Germany. We would give them a place to stay for as long as they needed. One couple went to the concentration camp and museum in Dachau before they came to visit us. There is a rather long walkway hedged by bushes to the entrance. One of them noticed what looked like money rolled up. They picked it up and discovered it was five hundred dollars.

Before spending several hours touring the campground, they reported their find to the museum owners, not specifying the amount. By the time they left, no one had reported losing any money. When they came and visited us, after a German breakfast, they said the Lord directed them to give us the money. We were ecstatic as it was the exact amount we needed for the piano lessons. They had even a more significant reason to practice; God was concerned about their piano lessons in American dollars.

We were joyful that we had been obedient to the Lord to open our home up. It was more blessed and joyous to give than to receive. Our children learned a valuable lesson on the power of prayer. The Bible says in Matthew 7:11, *"If we know to give good gifts to our children, how much more will our heavenly Father give good gifts to those who ask him."*

REFLECTIONS:

Communication has never been more accessible. With modern conveniences like cell phones and the internet, we have almost instant access to anyone!

Do you know that God was ahead of our time in communication? Long before smartphones and computers, we had access to our Heavenly Father through prayer! We grow and build our relationship with God through conversation with Him, in other words, through prayer.

Is communication with the Lord an ongoing part of your day? Be mindful of sharing your thoughts with Him throughout the day.

CHAPTER 16

TRANSPORTED

All things happen in divine time.
Mark 2:3

EVERY YEAR all our staff and our GIs would attend the Assembly of God Serviceman's retreat at Berchtesgaden, Germany. On one such occasion, we were asked to drop by and visit a fabulous missionary family doing radio ministry in Austria. I was reluctant as we had about a six-hour drive home to Bensheim. I really did not want to detour into Austria. Yet, we were so touched by their poverty that we left most of our personal belongings, coats, shoes, and some cash with them.

At about ten o'clock, after a powerful prayer meeting with them for their ministry and praying for their children, we departed to go to Bensheim. I made sure I had enough DM coins because the autobahn gas stations closed at night, and only coin-operated pumps remained open.

I was startled when I got to the Bensheim exit, thinking, "Oh, what a quick trip!"

...we realized we had been transported by God.

Upon looking at the clock, which read 11:00 p.m., and viewing those unused coins, we realized we had been transported by God. He had rewarded our kindness with a miracle like Philip experienced in Acts Chapter 8.

DIVINE MATCH MAKING

Prov 18:22, *"Whosoever finds a wife finds a good thing and obtains favor of the Lord."*

As mentioned before, The Assemblies of God held an annual servicemen's retreat in Berchtesgaden, Germany. One year we were boarding our VW vans, ready to head to a retreat, when we noticed that one of our staff members, Tim Thomas, was missing. Tim had come to our Bensheim Center several months prior and asked to join our team. He was a graduate of Oral Roberts University with a master's degree in Music and was touring Europe.

We were all in our vans, ready to go to Berchtesgaden, but Tim was missing. Tim wanted to stay behind, but the rule was that everyone would go. We persuaded him that it was a wonderful, powerful retreat. At that time, around five hundred or more military soldiers would be in attendance.

As Tim reluctantly entered the van, Sheryl encouraged him, saying, "Tim, you will have a wonderful time."

Tim replied, "I won't."

Margit was one of the van drivers, the one Tim rode in, as we traveled to the hotel. As God would have it, they began to talk to each other at the retreat and were married sometime later. Teasing Tim, later on, was always expressed in two words: "I won't!"

Margit, a dental assistant with a burning desire to work for Jesus, came to us at a great sacrifice and ministered for several years. In response to a critical financial need, she gave us her life savings of 9,000 Deutsche marks, about $5,263.00, to the ministry. She would later say she got a bargain—after all, where else could you get a husband for 9,000 Deutsche marks?

Tim and Margit have ministered in children's ministry and music ministry throughout Germany all their lives. They are an incredible couple, still serving God!

In those days, Margit was so precious to our children. She told them Bible stories and was a sweetheart! Our workload was hefty at Bensheim, and it was a Godsend that Margit did such a super job with the children.

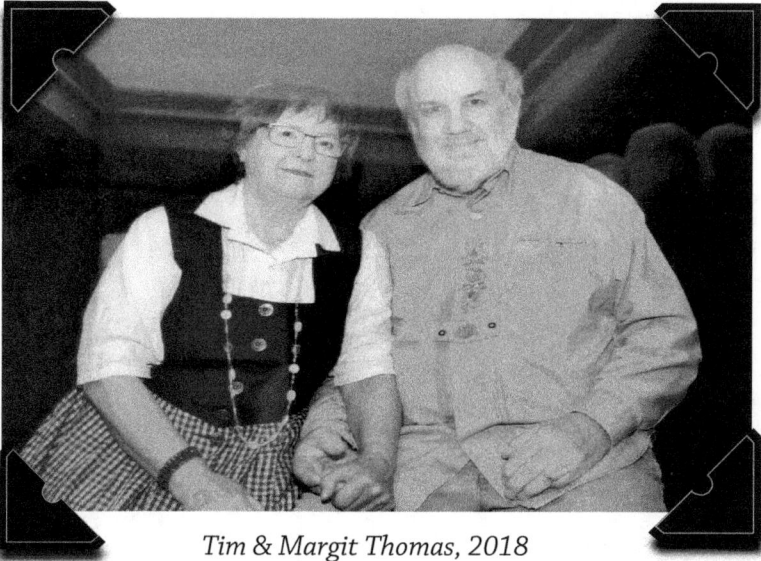

Tim & Margit Thomas, 2018

REFLECTIONS:

Since the days of Adam and Eve, God has proven to be an excellent matchmaker. Can you picture anyone better for Adam as he sat alone in the garden? Eve was literally the perfect mate.

Today, there is much pressure to find "the one." People take personality tests and submit lengthy bios statistically run through databases to find the right match. But as we trust more of our lives to Jesus, we shouldn't feel any burden in finding our spouse. God, in His infinite wisdom, has just the right companion for you. Do you believe and trust in that?

CHAPTER 17

A DIVINE HEALING
OF CANCER

For I am the Lord who heals you.
Exodus 15:26

In the summer of 1974, I began losing strength and weight. Finally, I went to the Heidelberg hospital; I remember standing in line with all the other foreigners who did not have the social medicine offered to German Nationals. A doctor, who I later found out was Dr. Uhl-the director at the University Hospital of Heidelberg, picked me out of the line and asked me to come to his personal office. He personally examined me and arranged for an immediate x-ray examination.

They injected fluid into my lymph node system and took twenty-eight x-rays. While showing us the x-rays, Dr. Uhl bluntly told us that I was terminally ill. He said the cancer was too far advanced and gave me about six months to live. At that time, I was only thirty-four years old, and we had three beautiful children.

Before leaving his office, I said, "Doctor, please document all the facts, as I believe God is going to heal me."

He wrote, "Either the patient is in total denial, or he has not grasped the gravity of his situation."

I quickly bottomed out at one-hundred twenty pounds. I was so weak that I would practically fall out of bed, then push myself up to a standing position.

Sheryl sent prayer requests to her many friends and acquaintances in ministry, literally living in all of the far-flung corners of the world. Thanks to her, there must have been thousands of people praying for me. Prayer cloths, special oil—you name it—were sent by loving, concerned ministers and missionaries.

MEDICAL PROCEDURES

The only medical procedure I had was the removal of an enlarged testicle the size of an orange. It had malignant cancer. Upon the removal, I lost a considerable amount of blood and was listed in critical condition. The hospital sent samples to three different labs, and the results came back, "burse artic," which in German means the worst possible cancer. I was so very sick and weak.

Sheryl said the German pastors in the area had invited us to come to their retreat for prayer. Right after the songs, a message came forth, "I am the Lord that will heal thee." Sheryl was weeping, as she knew this was a voice from Heaven to us!

Seven German pastors anointed me with oil and prayed in unison with a mighty surge of glorious faith and power. The roar of their affectional fervent prayer was astounding. God's Word says that this prayer avails much! In the Amplified Bible, James 5:16 says, "It releases mighty power which is dynamic in its working. "

106

The North Texas District Assemblies of God Executive Superintendents E.R. Anderson, J.T. Davis Missions Director, and Joe Adams, Sec. Treasurer fasted and prayed for three days for me. Brother Adams was a close friend, having married Sheryl and me. Somehow, they reached me at the remote retreat location! They told me they had been fasting and praying, and God had given them the assurance that I would live and not die. The scripture they gave me was "Rejoice, and again I say Rejoice." Philippians 4:4.

I gained strength back little by little, which I used for serving the Lord in any way I could. Several months later, I was up to my normal one-hundred, eighty pounds and operating at 100% capacity.

Four years later, just before going back to the U.S. I had a complete examination which lasted for several hours. Sheryl was in the waiting room telling everyone about how the Lord had healed her husband. She said that later she was getting very concerned about how long the examination was taking.

To the Glory of God, I have been in remission and divine health for over forty years.

They came to the conclusion that there was no cancer found. The doctors said I was in remission. To the Glory of God, I have been in remission and divine health for over forty years.

DR. UHL'S SECRETARY FROM HEIDELBERG UNIVERSITY HOSPITAL

Ps. 40:2-3, *"He brought me up out of a horrible pit. Many will see it and fear and will trust in the Lord."*

Twenty years later, while pastoring the Immanuel Assembly of God Church in Middleburg Heights, Ohio, we experienced an incredible verification and follow-up of my healing from cancer. A young man, who was the mascot for the Cleveland Browns football team, was powerfully drawn into our church by the Holy Spirit. He drove by several times and felt compelled to come in. He answered the altar call and was gloriously saved. He would jokingly say it was so fun to tell eighty-thousand football fans to pray at a critical juncture of the game.

This young man's aunt visited him from Germany; she did not know Christ, and he was concerned about her salvation. Sheryl invited him and his aunt for a delicious German meal with the ulterior motive of witnessing to her. At first, she harshly rebuffed us; she was very antagonistic toward spiritual things.

Then we told her about my cancer healing in Germany with Dr. Uhl at the Heidelberg University Hospital. She exclaimed very loudly, "Mein Gott," slapping her leg in great amazement! As it turns out, she was Dr. Uhl's secretary, and she remembered me. At the time of my surgery, she felt so very sorry for the young American couple with three small children and felt sure that this American man had passed away.

She stared at me with wonder and great amazement. God softened her heart, and we were able to lead her to a saving knowledge of Christ. With tears of great joy, we all rejoiced at God's ways that are higher than our ways as the heavens are above the earth. We were all awestruck that night at how God had brought all of these dynamics together in His perfect timing.

CHAPTER 18

RICKY AND SHARLA GET A MUCH-NEEDED TUTOR IN GERMAN SCHOOL

Satan meant it for evil, but God turned it around for good.

Genesis 50:20

WE HAD EXPERIENCED some anti-American sentiments throughout our time there, especially toward Ricky and Sharla in the German School system. One day it accelerated to a new level. Ricky was surrounded by some boys at school who were taunting him calling him, "Amy" (Pronounced Ah-me) for "American." It quickly escalated into fisticuffs resulting in some minor bruises. The school called, and we picked up Ricky immediately. He was no pushover.

When we returned home, Frau Swatung, the mother of Tobias, was at our door profusely apologizing for what her son had done to Ricky. She offered to tutor Ricky in her home down the street from our 100 Darmstader Str. home in Bensheim. After that, Ricky and Tobias became best of friends for the rest of our time in Germany.

Rick and Sharla made outstanding grades, with a great tutor for their German school work. Sheryl and I were very busy with the ministry and coffeehouses, so this was a tremendous blessing to have someone make sure the children got their homework done, as well as any other assistance they needed!

Frau Swatung also gave German classes for our staff members. She became a very dear friend to all our staff. Great will be her reward in heaven. This turned out to be a Roman 8:28 experience, "All things work together for good."

ICELANDIC AIRPORT MIRACLE

Isaiah 43:19, *"See, I will make a way in the wilderness."*

At one point, we felt led to make a trip back to the United States to raise funds. We prayed for the right timing. When we got the green light in prayer, we counted the varied European monies in our safe. At our Sunday meetings, we received offerings, including from people from all over Europe who were present. When we counted the various currencies, we had just enough for our round-trip tickets.

Upon arriving at the Luxembourg airport, we discovered the Icelandic flight had been canceled, so we got a voucher for a hotel and meals. We were so exhausted, as our work at the Bensheim center and the coffee house kept us very busy. I think we slept solidly until the following day.

God's timing was perfect.

When our flight landed in Iceland for a fuel stop, I noticed that a huge Saturn plane landed right behind us. Shortly after landing, while in the restroom, I began meeting ministers that I knew from the North Texas Assembly of God District. Sheryl experienced the same "chance" meeting. We booked several meetings right there at the Iceland Airport because we were at the right place at the right time. God's timing was perfect! We found out that our minister friends had made an unscheduled stop on the way home from a tour in Israel. We had some excellent "God planned" meetings while in Texas because of this airport encounter.

REFLECTIONS:

The word "luck" isn't a biblical concept. Instead, luck is a superstitious event that occurs outside of our control with significant impact. For example, we find a four-leaf clover and then believe that we will win the lottery.

Our God isn't manipulated through superstition. God operates through miracles—events that may be hidden from us but never a surprise to Him. What may seem like a random, chance encounter is always a God-ordained opportunity He allows and desires for us.

CHAPTER 19

CHARLIE SPRECKLES, TO THE RESCUE

---

*I will rejoice because you have rescued me.
I will sing to the Lord because He is so
good to me.*

Psalm 13:5-6

After several years in Germany, we had the opportunity to visit family and friends in the United States and raise much-needed support for our ministry in Bensheim. Sheryl and I landed in New York and took a train to our friend's home in Long Island. It was a cold evening when we arrived at a little station at Cold Spring Harbor. It was heated and well-lit, very cozy.

When our friend Charlie Spreckles arrived, he was shocked to see the heat and lighting. He said in all his years, he had

It was God's provision for two weary travelers.

never seen it open, heated, and lighted. It was God's provision for two weary travelers.

On the way to his house, he told me the transmission had gone out on his VW bug. So, I volunteered to fix it. He asked if his nephew John Kordon could help, telling me that John was "trying to find himself."

The next day while we put in a new transmission, I ministered to John, who was impressed that a preacher could also be a mechanic. We developed a bond and prayed together. (Years later, after graduation from Valley Forge Assemblies of God in Valley Forge in Pennsylvania, John became our Youth Pastor in Flemington, New Jersey. God works in mysterious ways, His wonders to perform!)

The next day Charlie volunteered to take us to the airport to continue our trip to Texas. Unfortunately, we did not have the money for the tickets but figured after he dropped us off, we could have Sheryl's mother arrange to purchase the tickets for us. However, Charlie insisted on seeing us off at the gate. I was embarrassed that he would find out we didn't have the tickets or money.

The traffic was fierce; we were running a bit late and had to hurry to the gate. At the last second, Charlie said, "Get in line. I'm paying for your tickets."

In the next couple of minutes, we found ourselves seated on the plane and praising God for the rapid and remarkable chain of events that had just taken place. It is always safe to trust the Lord even though sometimes we are trying to wing it ourselves. God always has a better way and will often surprise us with a miracle.

CHAPTER 20

TIMES OF CHANGE

To everything, there is a season, a time for every purpose under Heaven.

Ecclesiastes 3:1

SOMEONE ONCE SAID, "the one constant in life is change." Our seventh year in Germany was a year of change. Project transition was discontinued, and the Army was drastically drawing down the number of troops, even closing some bases. The owners of Bensheim graciously allowed us out of our contract, and we discontinued a couple of our coffee houses. We were reminded of the verses in Ecclesiastes 3 and looked forward to what God had for us next.

AN UNEXPECTED BLESSING

Ruth 2:16, *"Let fall also some of the handfuls on purpose for her."*

While this transition was happening, Chaplain Colonel Kalioma called and asked me to help him with a particular project which had never been done before. The Army wanted to decentralize its troop concentration for tactical reasons. So they rented a new high-rise building in two locations, Lampertheim and Oggersheim, to use as housing for the military. I would serve as the auxiliary Chaplain.

There would be a GS13 part-time salary for me and fifty dollars each service for Sheryl to play the organ. We were ecstatic. For the first time in seven years, we would have some personal monies and remain in our calling.

Chaplain Kalioma wanted me to make arrangements with local churches in these two towns to create chapel services. We had one service at 9:30 am and the other at 11:00 am on Sunday. We also had an Assembly of God Service at 6 pm in a facility we rented in downtown Mannheim. After one year, the chapel service held in a Lutheran church in Lampertheim grew to one-hundred thirty in attendance. The other service, held in an ecumenical church in Oggersheim, grew to ninety.

Most of the attendees got saved in our general protestant service. We could not do the traditional altar call, so we asked those who wanted prayer to stay behind after the benediction. Sometimes entire families would come to Christ together.

Ricky and Sharla were great missionaries, helping with the children. Ricky would set up a movie for the children's church, and Sharla was so sweet to the little ones. Parents loved the affection and care Ricky and Sharla gave their children. We always made sure we treated all three, Ricky, Sharla, and our little Liana, to ice cream on the base for their help at both chapel services.

I experienced something brand new once at a water baptism. A lady who had recently come to Christ gave a resounding testimony of what Jesus had done in her life and in the lives of her family. She was overjoyed and oh so thankful. When this lady came up out of the water, she spontaneously spoke in tongues, although she had no Pentecostal background. She reminded me of the blind man who said in effect, "I don't know about the theology of all this, I just know that once I was blind, but now, I see."

Because we were restricted in our general Protestant services, we taught the baptism in the Holy Spirit in our home groups. We experienced many miracles in response to our prayer in the Holy Spirit according to 1 Corinthians 14:15, "*I will pray in the spirit.*" When we left that ministry, our Lutheran pastor host, who was a gracious and godly man, said, "I have seen the book of Acts in action."

"I have seen the book of Acts in action".

REFLECTIONS:

Sometimes God closes doors and things to come to an end. This is not a time to be disappointed. Look forward with anticipation because God is opening new doors and opportunities.

The next time a door closes, what will you do? Be encouraged, looking forward to a better way—a blessed way!

CHAPTER 21

BEAUTIFUL DEANA MARIE

---

*Children are a gift from the Lord, and the
fruit of the womb is a reward.*

Psalm 127:3

ON FEBRUARY 7, 1977, God gave us our wonderful fourth child, Deana. She was born on Sheryl's birthday. Now, birthdays are a big deal in Germany! And this was also the beginning of our transition from Bensheim.

We had no money and no insurance. We had enough money for the hospital bill but no money for the doctor's bill. I had spent considerable time with Sheryl's doctor, discussing what he called "religion."

> *...birthdays are a big deal in Germany!*

The doctor called me into his office and told me there would be no bill from him. I was brushing away the tears of joy when I attempted to tell Sheryl the good news. She immediately went into panic mode, asking what was wrong with our baby.

I explained the doctor's wishes, and we were so thankful as we held our Deana for the first time—crying tears of joy for all the Lord had done for us.

After God had so wonderfully taken care of the doctor bill, we coined the phrase, "Dee Dee our free-be." She is now forty and such a blessing, especially because I never forgot Sheryl's birthday. Deana would always remind me: "It is Mom's and my birthday!"

REFLECTIONS:

Birthdays...Birthdays! A time of new life, new gifts, new miracles. The Word says in Isaiah 43:4 that *"You are precious and honored in my sight."* God rejoiced on the day you were born. Take time this year to reflect on the good gifts of life from God—even your own.

Prayer: God, thank you for this life you have given me. Help me to live as your child, born of God. In Jesus' name.

CHAPTER 22

THREE VISIONS CONFIRM GOD'S DIRECTION

While Peter thought about the vision, the Spirit spoke to him.

Acts 10:19

WE HAD BEEN "Missionaries by Faith" for eight years, depending on God for all our needs. God had never failed us, not once! Through the years, Superintendent E.R. Anderson had allowed Faith Missionaries on the field around the world. The new Superintendent felt it was best for all Faith Missionaries to come home and itinerate for their full support.

I was busy with Oggersheim and Lampertheim as an auxiliary chaplain, and Sheryl was the coordinator for the Mannheim Chapel with Chaplain Askew. We had never had it so good while in Germany. We began to cry out to God for His divine direction.

As we were praying for guidance, God gave Sheryl a three-part vision. First, the old city of Heidelberg flooded with the water lapping up against the Old Roman Bridge. Then, in the second part, an angel took us by the hand and led us around an unfinished, large church building that was being built. We looked into a lovely home in the third part, but it had cobwebs hanging everywhere and newspapers scattered all over the floor.

Three weeks later, just as Sheryl had described to me, the water was lapping up against the Old Roman Bridge for the first time in one hundred years. This was in 1978. Today, the high-water level plaque for "1978" is still visible at the end of the Heidelberg Old Roman Bridge.

Sheryl and I were convinced that this was a clear sign from God for us to pack up and return to the States. In addition, our two older children, Ricky and Sharla, were now approaching their teenage years, so it was a good time for them to return.

A Camping We All Will Go

Psalm 84:11, *"No good thing will He withhold from those who walk uprightly."*

Toward the end of our auxiliary chaplain's ministry, I wanted to take the family on a European tour before returning to the United States. While making a pastoral visit, I noticed a small camping trailer being used for an on-site construction office. The next day while checking on it, I discovered it had been vandalized, and they were hauling it off to the junkyard.

The man said, "You don't want this one, but I have a better one we are using as an office, which is available now."

I bought it for 500 DM. We cleaned it profusely inside and out and furnished it with new curtains and new flooring. The clerk laughed at me when I registered because he saw "Junk Yard" (Schrott Halle) on the old title. But we didn't care because that little trailer became a pleasant home for all six of us as we toured sixteen European countries over the next six weeks.

Upon leaving Germany, we gave it to a German missionary couple who then shipped it to the Philippines. God had plans for that resurrected "junkyard" trailer far beyond our expectations. God's ways are higher and more interesting than our ways as the heavens are above the earth. (Isaiah 55:9)

Chaplain Kalioma took a special love offering for our family from both churches, which more than paid for our trip. It was a glorious, fun, and unforgettable trip with our four children. We handed our Manheim coffeehouse and prison ministry over to Assemblies of God Missionaries Jerry and June Groom and returned to the states in June of 1978.

OUR STATE SIDE FAITH ADVENTURE

Matthew 6:33, *"Seek first the Kingdom of God, and His righteousness and all these things will be given to you."*

We came home to the United States and were staying with Sheryl's family in Waxahachie, Texas. I had no job, no income, and four kids and a wife. I went to Sheryl's grandma's house, who was in Michigan. I fasted for three days and waited on the Lord for direction.

We loaded our belongings in a car we could pay cash for and headed to New Jersey. We talked to Superintendent Paproski of the New Jersey District of the Assemblies of God. He asked us to bring a small church into the Assemblies of God.

We had very little money but were determined to buy a small starter home. In the meantime, we were living in the

Sunday school rooms in the basement of the church. God gave Sheryl a vision of a man's face while we were in prayer. It was Mr. Pardin, one of our deacons.

God also spoke to us and said, "If you take care of my business, I will take care of your business." So we immediately got up and went door to door, inviting people to our church.

Mr. Pardin called and asked us to meet him at a particular address in the morning. Our excitement waned when we saw the house. Sheryl had already looked at it, and the home was too expensive for us. We soon discovered that not only was the house drastically reduced in price because of estate problems, but Mr. Pardin had talked to the banker telling him he would sign for us.

"If you take care of my business, I will take care of your business."

When I sat down with the banker, he asked, "Reverend, what is your salary?"

I said, "Fifty dollars per week and all the garden vegetables we can eat!"

He said, "I was afraid of that, but Mr. Pardin has already made arrangements!" We got the house!

REFLECTIONS:

Once you hear from God, stepping out in faith always takes courage: Courage to believe before fully knowing. Courage to act without completely seeing.

Focus your mind on ways you have or *will* have to believe in God's guiding hand and provision. Write them down and then step out in total faith.

CHAPTER 23

FAITHFUL ADVENTURES IN MEXICO – TO THE GERMAN COMMUNITY

A man from Macedonia pleaded with Paul, saying, "Come over to Macedonia and help us."

Acts 16:9

IN 1979, ASSEMBLIES OF GOD Missionary Cooper sent out an urgent call for some German-speaking people to minister to the Mennonites in Cuauhtemoc, Mexico. Their young people were drifting away from the church and getting into drugs, etc.

Cuauhtemoc was in Missionary Cooper's jurisdiction, but he did not speak German. The German District Assemblies of God Superintendent Raymond Reub contacted me about making an exploratory missionary trip. We decided to use our vacation time for the occasion.

Accompanied by Sheryl's parents, they drove their new Buick in the mud holes and over the streams, hills, and valleys. We couldn't help but laugh at all the fun and adventure we were all having. Missionary Cooper met us at the border and guided us through the border crossings.

In Cuauhtemoc, we were on our own. The first thing we did was go to the nearest general store, which was also a meeting point for the entire region. While gathering information and handing out tracts, we met Mr. Enns, who invited us to his home and farm. He was the perfect contact person, a godly man who was very concerned about his community.

Mr. Enns arranged for several meetings in homes and schools. We had brought literature in German, our musical instruments, my trumpet, Sheryl's accordion, and some Moody Science films about God's creation in German. Our meetings consisted of singing, using the song sheets in German. This was followed by a brief message, the film, and always an altar call at the conclusion.

He was the perfect contact person, a godly man...

Our best asset was our son Ricky who was fourteen years old and spoke the dialect of the German Mennonites. In our meetings, he would interpret, witness, and pray with the people. My mother-in-law also spoke their dialect and prayed with the ladies.

In one meeting at a schoolhouse, the men sat on one side and the ladies on the other. At the altar call, I asked the people who wanted to be born again to remain seated while the others were dismissed. Everyone stayed and came to know Jesus as their Savior. They were so sweet and thankful. After this, we were invited into many of the homes. Most of them had fifteen to twenty children.

In just a few days, a Pentecostal church was born. We made a request to Missionary Cooper for a full-time missionary to come as soon as possible. We had the names and addresses of those who truly were born again and wanted further ministry. We sent a group of AIMer's to help with the church building program. Our son Ricky and our youth pastor were among the first to help with establishing a church for all the new converts.

Soon a church building was purchased. Years later, our Youth Pastor at Immanuel church went to pastor the now thriving church. Mike Hadinger had grown up in a German-speaking church in Ohio. He and his wife, Ilona, are still in Mexico, ministering to Spanish and German-speaking people in Mexico.

The only negative part of this trip was that we all got a severe case of Montezuma's revenge, but we all survived. Our churches in New Jersey and Ohio made several mission trips to help during the subsequent years, and our churches gave mission offerings to help.

REFLECTIONS:

Seeing God work is a joyous experience—God's Holy Spirit working in a moment or an entire season, as people come to Salvation. When was a time or season when the Lord empowered you in a way that was life-changing? God wants to do that again and propel you into a deeper faith. Even today!

Prayer: Lord, begin a new work in me so that your salvation may be seen through me. Even today, Lord.

CHAPTER 24

MOVING FROM LITTLE FALLS, NEW JERSEY CHURCH (CALVARY ASSEMBLY)

Whoever looks into the perfect law of liberty and continues in it, and is not a forgetful hearer, but is a doer of the Word, this man will be blessed in his deed.

James 1:25

WE HAD PURCHASED a lovely little four-bedroom house which I completely remodeled. We removed the plastic tiles in the kitchen and bathrooms and all the old, ugly handmade cabinets. I looked for a cabinet shop and found one that a young Jewish man owned; I used the opportunity to witness to him. He was so kind and gave me cabinets to doll up our new home.

God blessed our home project in many ways. A young lady, who was an alcoholic, got saved at our church. Her family owned an Italian imported tile company. She was delighted to give us our choice of beautiful Italian tile for both bathrooms. A couple of ladies from the church wanted to put new carpeting in our home. Sheryl was modest and picked out the cheapest. But they insisted on buying top-of-the-line, beautiful carpet for the home.

The house had a lovely, fenced backyard. A Greek family lived next door and owned a huge swimming pool. The wife always had our children over for Greek food and swimming parties. We were able to pray for her and her young son, who was Rick's age.

The dietician in charge of school lunches noticed that Rick and Sharla always ate their entire dinner. She talked to Rick, who explained that we were pastoring the Little Falls Church, and his dad didn't make much money. From then on, every Friday, she would deliver fruits, lasagna, fresh vegetables, and pretzels from the cafeteria to our home. We were so blessed!

A year later, we moved after completing our assignment. Church attendance was about ninety people. We had purchased our home for $48,000 and were able to sell it for $67,000. God was blessing us for our sacrifices.

FLEMINGTON ASSEMBLY OF GOD CHURCH

Matthew 7:11, *"If you then, being evil, know how to give good gifts to your children, how much more will your Father who is in heaven give good things to those who ask him."*

Superintendent Paproskie arranged for us to pastor the Flemington Assembly of God Church. Here we were to experience the fruition of the remaining parts two and three of Sheryl's earlier vision (see Chapter 22).

At Flemington, we moved into the parsonage, which was built onto the church. We had such rapid growth that our parsonage was used for a nursery, church offices, and Sunday School rooms. I removed the ugly cabinets and took out the old bathroom fixtures there, as well. And I repaired the bathroom upstairs, which was so plugged that there was no running water.

Here we would experience the fruition of Sheryl's earlier vision.

The wallpaper was in such poor condition that I removed it and painted all the rooms. New flooring was installed next in all the rooms, as well as new light fixtures. After remodeling the interior, we cleaned up the yard, which looked like a jungle, and planted some plants. But the house was so crowded, as it was being used for both home and church facilities, we felt that we must find a home for our four precious children.

PART TWO OF THE VISION GIVEN TO SHERYL IN GERMANY

In looking for a house, God directed us to the Broadview Estates near Flemington. One place was overgrown and obviously not occupied. The owner told us a woeful tale of eviction, litigation, and damage to the home. Upon opening the front door, Sheryl, in amazement said, "I saw this exact house and scene in my vision."

We were able to buy the house at an almost giveaway price and closed on a handshake because of the ongoing litigation. Mr. Lovavy paid for the utilities for three months and allowed us to repair the house while it was in litigation. Five years later, we doubled our money when we sold that home.

REFLECTIONS:

The Bible talks about a "double-blessing" in Isaiah 61:7. What does a double portion blessing mean? It is God giving you double for the sacrifice or shame you have endured on His behalf.

To receive a double portion, one must believe and expect a blessing beyond their own capability. Look back at the good things in life and count those as blessings. Now look to today, no matter what you face. When you turn the situation over to God, He always brings blessings. Expect them. Rejoice in them.

CHAPTER 25

A MODERN-DAY JERICHO MARCH FOR VICTORY!

I have given Jericho into your hand. March around the city.

Joshua 6:2-3

WE WERE PLANNING a building program shortly after we arrived in Flemington, New Jersey. But when we applied for a building permit, we hit a brick wall. The town council insisted we deposit an exorbitant amount of money in escrow to ensure we would finish the site work. As a result, we had $50,000 to start our faith venture-building program and were in a dilemma.

One day, God spoke to me and said, "Have a Jericho March around the land." So on Saturday, I had some of our men mow a path around the entire five acres. Then, in the first and second services, I announced we would be having a Jericho march immediately after the second service.

Almost everyone from both services showed up, and we had a shouting, singing, praising time, complete with tambourines, trumpets, and wonderful praises from an excited church! We marched around the property several times. We knew, by faith, that God was going to allow us to build a place of worship for His Glory.

Early Monday morning, as I was just waking up. the Lord said, "Go get your building permit!" So I went to the appropriate office and, matter-of-factly, asked for the building permit. The clerk filled a blank one out with a marker, presented it to me, and said, "Twenty-five dollars, please."

This experiment is still functioning today!

Nothing more was ever said about the escrow, and of course, we didn't ask! God did a miracle for us in a low-key and almost nonchalant way. The Lord also provided an engineer and architect, Les Avery, to design and build our church. He worked for RCA, and they gave him the time off to work on the Flemington Church.

We had 18,000 feet of solar collectors for heating which was an experiment for Les Avery's company. The heating bills were very minimal. This experiment is still functioning today! We had the privilege of visiting with Les and Jeanie Avery in late 2017 and enjoyed remembering the good times we had shared in Flemington, where we saw God work in so many beautiful ways.

THIRD PART OF THE VISION GIVEN TO SHERYL IN GERMANY

Number 23:19, *"God is not a man that He should lie, nor the Son of Man that he should repent. Has He not spoken, and will He not make it good?"*

The third part of the vision was completed in a building program shortly after we arrived. The steel girders were up, but we had run out of money. I called a board meeting for special prayer, believing for the funds needed for the steel beams. Sheryl reminded the board and me about the vision she had in Germany. She told them of how the angel of the Lord had led us around a sizeable unfinished church and said, "It will be finished, not to worry." Sheryl felt we should praise the Lord, and so we began to do just that!

The very next morning, at this most critical juncture, an anonymous certified check appeared under my office door—praise be to God! This gift allowed us to complete our new church building in Flemington. It is located on Highway 202 on the hill for all to see. And it's a one-of-a-kind solar energy church. God was faithful to the powerful vision! In 2017, I was privileged to preach there again, and I recounted this story to the congregation. All Glory to God!

Flemington New Jersey Church

Another view of the Flemington New Jersey Church

REFLECTIONS:

Giving thanks to God is ALWAYS—ALWAYS the best strategy. When you are unsure, give thanks to God. The prophet Isaiah often referred to "Jehovah," a Hebrew name for God, meaning "I am who I am." The name Jehovah is often paired with an additional name to declare the complete goodness of God

For example, He is Jehovah and WILL provide. When you are sick, give thanks to God. He is Jehovah Rapha, the God who heals. Give thanks to Jehovah Adonai, who is the master of all things. Live victoriously through our Jehovah.

CHAPTER 26

A MIRACLE IN THE BUSY TOWN OF LONDON, ENGLAND

The Lord will make a way where there seems to be no way.

Isaiah 43:16

IN 1984 WE TOOK A FAMILY TRIP back to Germany to revisit some of the sentimental locations and visit old friends. This was just before we assumed the pastorate of Immanuel Assembly of God in Middleburg Heights, Ohio.

Rick and Sharla had just graduated from high school. We had given Sharla a rather expensive Seiko watch for her graduation. We stayed overnight in a hotel in London after we landed. The next morning, we were setting out to take a city tour. We boarded a very crowded train from our hotel to the train station in downtown London. To Sharla's horror, she discovered she had lost her watch either on the train or in the crowded train station. We frantically looked to no avail for her watch. She was in tears. There were thousands of people everywhere.

Heavy-hearted, we took the city double-decker tour through the city. It was evening, and we returned to the train station. At that point, the Lord spoke to Sheryl and said, "Check the lost and found."

She saw a tiny sign hanging over the lost and found. The man there said that no one ever turns in anything of value. But Sheryl, having heard from the Holy Spirit, was insistent that there was a Seiko watch that had been turned in. At that very moment, a lady walked in, and Sheryl said, "Did you find a Seiko watch?"

[We] both began praising God for an absolute miracle.

The lady was startled and showed us the watch. Sharla and I both began praising God for an absolute miracle. It was like finding a needle in the haystack.

I witnessed to the gentleman and the lady about the power of God to help in time of need and that this meant so much to Sharla. They were very impressed, especially at our shouts of joy! We thanked God for the honest person who had turned in the watch.

A ONCE IN A LIFETIME TRIP TO SOUTH AFRICA

Ps 72:18, *"Praise the Lord God, the God of Israel, who alone does such wonderful things."*

While pastoring Immanuel in Middleburg Heights, Ohio, we were very blessed to add a family from South Africa to our church. They were Mom and Dad Hofmeister and their extended family.

For our thirty-fifth anniversary, Mr. Hofmeister arranged a trip to South Africa for us. In Johannesburg, we met Mr. Hofmeister's son and his wife. They pastored an Assemblies of God church in Johannesburg. They treated us royally as we traveled, preached in seven churches, including a permanent tent church in Johannesburg. They took us on a guided African Safari, and we were so blessed to stay in their time-share hotels with fabulous South African food. In addition, they were excellent home-grown tour guides as we visited Cape Town and many other places of tremendous interest.

We were humbled and blessed by their kindness in making our thirty-fifth anniversary so very special. Again, we were reminded of Proverbs 10:22 *"The blessing of the Lord brings true riches, and he adds no sorrow with it, for it comes as a blessing from God."*

REFLECTIONS:

From lost watches to anniversaries, our daily living is important to God. These life experiences are avenues for the Holy Spirit to travel in us and through us. Through all of the many ways the Holy Spirit works, the one common goal is always to be more like Jesus.

Prayer: *Lord, keep me mindful of you in all things great and small. Thank you for guiding me, walking beside me, and loving me. May your Holy Spirit fill me up and always keep me close to you.*

CHAPTER 27

OUR SON RICK, A MISSIONARY TO GERMANY, CHOOSES A WIFE

For the Lord sees not as man sees. For man looks on the outward appearance, but the Lord looks at the heart.

1 Samuel 16:7

WHILE WE WERE PASTORING the Immanuel Assembly of God Church in Middleburg Heights, Ohio, our son Rick went to Germany as a missionary in training. He would be involved in church planting and university ministry in Munich, Germany. After a couple of years, he invited us to meet his girlfriend.

Sheryl was skeptical. Minna, a young Finnish lady, had very short blond hair and an equally short skirt. Minna was a model for Mercedes Auto shows and an airline attendant for Lufthansa. Because of Sheryl's Pentecostal upbringing, some of this set off alarms. We had both prayed for years for Rick's future companion. Things were very tense during a fantastic meal Sheryl had prepared for us.

After the meal, Rick asked us to come into the living room. Rick and Minna sat together on the love seat while Sheryl and I sat on the couch. Minna and Rick were bracing for the ensuing conversation. At that very moment, God gave Sheryl a vision. In the image, Minna was obviously pregnant. God said, "Minna will bear your son's children." That was that— plain and simple, case closed. You don't argue with God.

Rich was astonished that Sheryl was very content and happy with the idea of Minna as a prospective daughter-in-law. He asked Sheryl, and she told Rick that God had spoken, and she had nothing to say! Rick relayed this to Minna, and they had a big laugh for joy!

That was that plain and simple case closed.

They married about a year later. After several years, Minna became very concerned because she had been unable to conceive. Minna called Sheryl from Germany and was sobbing and crying, saying she could not get pregnant. Minna was overwhelmed with fear. At that moment, Sheryl recalled the vision and, with complete confidence, told Minna, "You will bear Rick's children, plural. God told me so."

Rick and Minna have been married twenty-five years and are the proud parents of two wonderful girls, Kristiina and Stephanie. They both attend Gordon Conwell University in Boston, Massachusetts. We affectionately call Minna our "daughter-in-love." Rick and Minna are both thoroughly Pentecostal missionaries.

Rick and Family

REFLECTIONS:

Hearing from God brings confidence. Even in situations that seem untenable. But when He pierces your heart and mind, stand on his word. He has spoken and will bring it to pass.

Remain steadfast and confident no matter the circumstances. Keep moving forward in faith, and you will witness the mighty work of God.

CHAPTER 28

MIRACLES WITH THE YOUTH IN PORTIRAFTE, GREECE

This kind does not go out except by fasting and prayer.

Matthew 17:21

IN ONE OF OUR MANY short-term mission trips back to Europe, we preached at an Assemblies of God Youth Camp in Portirafte, Greece. At first, we were met with tremendous spiritual opposition from the young people in their twenties.

I felt the Lord request that we fast and pray for a breakthrough. Slowly during the next few days, we saw gradual changes. I continued to only fast, pray, sleep, and preach.

In the meantime, Sheryl would counsel those who came to her. It often seemed like all of them were into immorality; some had gotten abortions; others were into pornography, etc. Occasionally Sheryl would bring one of the precious young people to me, and we would offer prayers of deliverance over them.

The last night we experienced a deluge of God's mighty saving and delivering presence and power. The whole group was on their face crying out to God. What a miracle of God's saving, redeeming grace!

Sheryl bought candles for each of the young Greek people who would declare their new life in Christ. They would take a candle, and by doing so, would proclaim that they would let their light shine for Christ and be a mighty witness to others. As they lit their candle, they gave mighty testimonies of God's saving power and made commitments to continue to serve Jesus.

We were invited back the following year for the Youth Camp in Porto Rafti, Greece. Again, we had a Pentecostal revival together!

STAND BY FOR FLIGHT TO ENGLAND FOR A REVIVAL

Philippians 1:12, *"But I want you to know brothers that the things which happened to me have resulted in advancing the gospel."*

We came off that tremendous high of a God-breakthrough with the Greek young people, only to get detained at the Athens Airport. Because our daughter Liana worked in the HR Office at Continental Airlines, we would always fly standby. So, all the next day, we found ourselves standing by while the planes took off.

The next day our situation became even more desperate because we would soon be late for our revival in Lakenheath, England. So, all morning and into the afternoon, we simply "stood by."

The World Games were taking place in Athens, and the planes were overbooked with passengers. We did not have a purchased ticket, only stand-by status. The situation was impossible. We could not even buy a ticket because of the overbooking. I told Sheryl I would get us something to eat and disappeared around the corner.

While sitting on the bench, two young girls approached Sheryl, asking her the time. One of them twisted Sheryl's arm supposedly to get a better look at her watch. The other girl grabbed Sheryl's purse and ran with it. I am confident that Sheryl made a 100-yard dash record as she collided with the Albanian girl at the entrance door!

Then the fight started. The girl was kicking, pushing, hitting, and trying to get out the door with all her might. Sheryl was hanging on to her purse for dear life.

About that time, I came around the corner and heard a loud cry, "Richard!!!" I bolted to Sheryl, grabbed the girl's arm, and immediately the airport security was there. In the meantime, an American teenager chased down the other girl in the parking lot. She hid under the car, and he pulled her out, with her kicking and screaming. This absolutely made his day! He had the biggest grin on his face when he turned her over to the Airport Security.

Immediately we went from "zero" to "hero."

Immediately we went from "zero" to "hero." Seems these two girls had terrorized the airport for a couple of days before our encounter and had continued to get away with these kinds of acts. The airport officials asked what they could do for us.

Of course, we asked for a flight to England. Within an hour, we boarded the plane and were treated like celebrities. God works in mysterious ways, His wonders to perform.

We landed in England, with great thanks for divine intervention that had given us two seats on the plane. And, we had a tremendous revival meeting in England with two of our spiritual kids, Assembly of God missionaries Diane and Pat Green.

REFLECTIONS:

Have you ever experienced a long delay when traveling? Did it cause frustration, or were you at peace about the situation?

When you travel using God's map, you are always in the right place at the right time (God's time). Of course, we may not always know why we are waiting for this or delayed due to that. But by trusting God in His divine wisdom, we are right where we need to be.

Perhaps He is protecting us and keeping us safe. Or, the Lord may have us where we are to help someone else. So, if you are getting frustrated with delays, relax and be at peace. Trust God in His time.

CHAPTER 29

MINISTRY AT THE BIBLE SCHOOL IN UKRAINE

Preach the Word, be ready in season and out of season, reprove, rebuke, and exhort with all patience and teaching.

2 Timothy 4:2

SHERYL AND I WERE INVITED to minister at the Bible School in Ukraine. Several churches had come together to hold a short-term Bible School. Unfortunately, the church location was seriously overcrowded. In addition, they had a bank of outhouses which stank terribly!

To beat the system, Sheryl asked the pastor for the key to his private toilet. She thought surely it was a running toilet and was so proud to show me the key. She was also chagrined to find out that location was among the other outhouses and the only difference was a toilet seat nailed in place. We had a great time laughing at her find. What luxury!

From nine in the morning until late in the evening, we ministered intensely all week at the school. This is because these precious Ukrainians were so hungry for the Word. We also taught on marital relations, as they had absolutely no teaching on this subject. They mainly asked us many Biblical questions on marriage. We prayed for the couples.

What a beautiful sight to see the love of God showered down on them. Tears of joy flowed freely! God was doing great work! We were amazed at their tenacity in prayer and fervent worship and completely fell in love with them.

They had to endure many hardships as they had no running water and carried the water in buckets. The food supply was scarce. Yet, our hearts were moved at their joy—amid all their pain and poverty.

A MIRACLE ON THE WAY TO THE KIEV AIRPORT

Ps 9:10, *"There shall no evil befall you, neither shall any plague come near your tent."*

On the way from Eastern Ukraine to the Airport in Kiev, we experienced a miracle. The car we were riding in ran over a wrench, which flipped up, causing one end to puncture the gas tank, while the other end could be heard dragging on the road. The driver stopped to look at it and then shouted to get out and run away from the car. Sparks caused by the wrench that had been dragging, plus the leaking gas, could have caused ignition and possibly an explosion on the full tank of gas.

God had so miraculously protected us. He had a plan. The driver let all the gas drain out before we got near the car. He waved down another car and had a wrecker bring us to a makeshift, antiquated auto repair shop where they repaired the gas tank.

While they were fixing the car, we were busy witnessing to the other workers through our interpreter. Then, finally, we were able to lead them to Christ. Tears of joy ran down their faces. There were so thrilled to hear the loving message of a Christ that died for their sins. We then understood Satan meant to destroy us, but God had turned this situation around for His Glory!

FREE FIREWOOD FROM CLEVELAND WOOD PRODUCTS

Ephesians 3:20, *"Now to him who can do exceedingly beyond all we ask or imagine, according to the power that works in us. To Him be the glory in the church."*

Upon assuming the pastorate of Immanuel Assembly of God in Middleburg Heights, Ohio, I purchased a fireplace insert after receiving a special birthday offering from our wonderful congregation. The offering of $450 was just enough to buy a heater that I had on lay-a-way.

Rick and I would cut firewood together on one of our member's acreage. It was a great father-son activity, which saved us a lot of money on our heating bill. We had a lovely beautiful four-bedroom colonial home with a built-out basement.

Rich had just left to go to Germany as a Missionary in Training. I was sort of complaining to the Lord about missing him and those pleasant times of working together. Unfortunately, not only do missionaries sacrifice, but families who remain behind do too.

One day while driving back from a hospital visit, the Holy Spirit spoke very forcefully to me and said, "Look over there, that's where you are going to get your firewood." I looked to my left and saw a building and a sign, which read "Cleveland Wood Products." I immediately turned around and went inside. I introduced myself and asked if they had scraps to get rid of. They did not give me a clear answer, so I left my card with them. Then, a few days later, they called to tell me they had four pallets of wood for me!

I rented a truck, and they loaded up the wood with a forklift when I got there. Now, these were no ordinary irregular wood scraps. These were kiln-dried, hard–rock maple spindles made for vacuum cleaner brushes that either had machine flaws or were obsolete. The spindles would burn so clean I didn't have to empty the ashes and came packed in boxes that fit perfectly into my wonderful wood stove. I would go home and put a whole box of wood in with no fuss and no muss! Sheryl could even put the box in when needed.

One year I heated the house only with wood. The gas company man came to see if I was somehow by-passing the meter. We were able to show him the boxes of spindles in our extra-large garage, stacked and ready to burn. It kept our large colonial home toasty warm.

He went back with a good report that we were honest and blessed!

We were able to give the gas man a marvelous testimony of God's provision. He went back with a good report that we were honest and blessed! I continued to get the wood from Cleveland Wood Products for fourteen years until we resigned from Immanuel.

God is concerned about everything in our lives. Psalms 37:23 says, *"The steps of the righteous man are ordered of the Lord, and he delighted in his way."* I often recall the impactful "order" the Holy Spirit gave me that day to look toward the wood company.

Ministering to the students in Ukraine

REFLECTIONS:

Occasionally we host pity parties, but they typically aren't productive. On the other hand, hardship or disappointments can often be opportunities. So instead of feeling sorry for yourself, or having a negative thought about your situation, listen to see what the Lord may be telling you.

Be reminded: *For those that love the Lord, He will use all things for good.* Romans 8:28

CHAPTER 30

OPTING FOR ANOTHER FAITH VENTURE TO GERMANY

According to your faith

let it be done to you.

Matthew 9:29

AFTER SIXTEEN WONDERFUL YEARS, we resigned as pastors of the Immanuel Assembly in Middleburg Heights, Ohio, and opted for another faith venture to Germany. Shortly after leaving, we received an invitation to fill in as Missionaries to the military ministry of Ken Kraig in Wiesbaden, Germany.

We had just bought a new home in Houston, Texas, and were in the process of moving in when we received the call to come to Germany much earlier than we had expected. We were so very excited! Deana, our youngest daughter, was living with us at the time and had an excellent job with

Continental Airlines in the Human Resources office. Everyone loved her, and she loved her work.

One night as Sheryl lay in bed, the Holy Spirit said, "Get out of bed and dance for joy! Deana is coming to Germany with you." At first, Sheryl said, "But God, my husband, and Dee are sound asleep."

God spoke again. Sheryl jumped out and shouted for joy, speaking in tongues. Deana came running and said, "Mom, what is the matter?"

Sheryl said, "God just said you are going with us to Germany!"

Deana broke down and said, "I was just hoping and waiting for you to ask me."

Wow, how we thanked God for that night, as Dee took excellent care of all the children at the military church. She was our secretary. She designed and decorated the coffee house in Landstuhl better than Starbucks. God gave it the name "His Grounds Coffee House." She organized our music until her "Mr. Right," Charlie Morton, came along. She also helped Dittmar and Elisabeth Middlestadt as their secretary for Lydia Magazine. Deana was called by God, and what a blessing to our church ministry and the Coffee House.

Greg Mundez, the regional European Director, asked us to pastor the Assemblies of God Military Church in Ramstein, Germany. Sheryl and I went door to door throughout the military village giving fliers about the Assembly of God church service at the Vogelweh Military Chapel-serving Kaiserslautern, Landstuhl, and Ramstein area. What glorious services were held, as we provided a full-service program for our incredible military.

A COFFEE HOUSE IS BORN IN LANDSTUHL

Matthew 7:7, *"Ask and it will be given to you, seek, and you will find, knock, and it will be opened to you."*

We had many fond memories at our coffee house ministries during our first faith adventure in Germany. We spent time in prayer, asking God for His clear direction. We asked if this was His will for us that we would find either a closed door or an open door on our first day looking for a coffee house.

Early one Saturday morning, Sheryl, Ulla (a wonderful Christian woman from Wiesbaden), and I set out to find a coffee house. We drove through various parts of Landstuhl and ended up on the main street. Suddenly, we spotted a storefront that had its windows papered over.

We peeked in and saw Karl, the owner who let us in. Immediately, we knew this would be an excellent place for a coffee house! So, we told him we wanted to rent the space. But he informed us there were other interested parties.

Suddenly Sheryl became very bold with Karl. She poked him on his chest and very authoritatively said, "They are not here, but we are, and we are ready to sign."

They are not here, but we are, and we are ready to sign.

We explained how we wanted to minister to hurting nationals and to our U.S. Military. Later, Karl told us he had worked in the Catholic Church with drug addicts and had never seen anyone delivered. We were able to share with him powerful testimonies of young people set free by the divine power of Almighty God. Karl ultimately became a wonderful friend of ours. Often his wife made us fabulous German cakes and cookies while we were working on the coffee house. That particular day, we went up to his apartment and immediately signed the papers.

I tore down walls, put in two bathrooms, updated everything necessary for an awesome coffee house. The best room was dedicated for use as a Prayer Room. The coffee house served as a meeting place for church fellowships, ladies' meetings, street evangelism, and a starting place for a pioneer German Church.

Landstuhl Coffee House, decorated by our daughter, Deana

An Angelic Vision

Hebrews 13:2, *"Do not forget to show hospitality to strangers, for by so doing some people have shown hospitality to angels unawares."*

One freezing, blustery, snowy evening, only Sheryl and I showed up at the coffeehouse. I went into the Prayer Room while Sheryl covered the coffee house. No one was coming in, so she went out on the streets to talk to people, and hand out tracts and invite them in. She was shivering and extremely cold when she came in and sat down to warm herself. Naturally, she felt disappointed and somewhat dejected.

A very nice-looking silver-haired elderly lady came in and sat down at Sheryl's table. She put her hand on Sheryl's arm and asked, "What's the matter?"

Sheryl said, "No one is here."

The lady said, "You are here, I am here, and God is here. And God is pleased with your work for Him."

Sheryl was overwhelmed by the lady's intense presence. After Sheryl came to her senses, the lady had disappeared. We were convinced she was an angel giving great encouragement to a weary worker. The next night, the place was packed with G.I.'s. People came in off the street to find Christ as their Savior.

REFLECTIONS:

Walking by faith has ups and downs and requires persistence. But we should never give up on God's word. Always believe that He will come and minister to you, even in your darkest hour. That is His promise! Thank God for the loving-kindness of His son, even on our cloudy days. A miracle is on the way.

CHAPTER 31

A PROPHETIC WORD OVER OUR DEANA

Do not quench the Spirit,

do not despise prophecies.

1 Thessalonians 5: 19-20

DEANA WAS EXPERIENCING some medical difficulties and received a dire medical prognosis from a German specialist. She was devastated, and so we were as her parents. Deana was going to miss the church service because she felt so down. But her faith kicked in, and she came to minister to the children at the Vogelweh Military Church.

After the service, as she was coming upstairs, a lady named Flora asked Sheryl where her daughter was. This was only the second time Flora had been to our church, and she said she had a Word from the Lord. Immediately Flora placed her hand on Deana's tummy and said, "What the doctor told you about today— I, the Lord, am healing you!"

The prophecy went on to say that God had a wonderful young man for Deana and that He loved God with all his heart. He had followed God since he was a youth, and he was musical. Finally, Flora concluded by saying that Deana and God's gift of a husband would serve God and others together. Sheryl and Deana were both in tears at the incredibly powerful prophecy to her dire need.

Sheryl and I took Deana back to the German specialist. He was astounded. Sheryl said she shouted "Hallelujah," when the doctor said he had witnessed a miracle. God had healed Deana and had a wonderful man prepared for her future.

It was love at first sight. At the dedication of our coffeehouse that Deana had worked so hard on and decorated, Charlie walked into Deana's life. It was love at first sight! Six months later, they were married.

In response to her remarkable healing, Deana was able to have two precious children, Charlie and Julia. Charlie is a Major in the Air Force, a super Dad, a church musician, a worship leader, a great Bible teacher, an outstanding husband, and a great son-in-law to us! We are so thankful Deana obeyed God to come to Germany to find God's choice for a wonderful husband!

HEIDELBERG CASTLE WEDDING FOR LIANA AND JOE IN GERMANY

Psalms 25:12- 13, *"Who are those who fear the Lord? He will show them the path they should choose. They will live in prosperity and their children will inherit the land". (NLB)*

Through God-directed circumstances, our middle daughter, Liana, met Joe. Joe was Chief Pilot for Continental Airlines, and Liana was in the Continental Airlines Human Resources office, where they met and fell in love. Joe and Liana had flight privileges with the airline and came to visit us in Germany. Joe said, "Dad keep a secret, don't tell your wife. I want to surprise Liana at the top of the Eifel Tower in France with an engagement ring."

Joe and Liana went to the top of the Eifel Tower, where he totally surprised Liana with an engagement ring! When they rejoined us, we were all crying and rejoicing with great joy. Joe's Mom called Liana, "Lovely Liana." She stated she had been praying for Joe to have a wonderful Christian wife. Sheryl and I had also prayed diligently for her future companion.

They were married in a storybook wedding in the Heidelberg Castle in Germany, complete with a pipe organ to shake the whole castle and trumpeters! Liana was born in Heidelberg, so it was extraordinary that she could be married there. In addition, all of Liana's and Joe's coworkers could come to Germany, as they worked for Continental Airlines and were able to attend a God-planned wedding. I have had the wonderful privilege of officiating in all four of our children's weddings.

We continued to pastor the Ramstein Military church for six years. We then returned to Texas. Upon our return there, we continued to minister in various capacities, including interim pastoring.

Charlie's Promotion to Air Force Major
Charlie, Deana, Little Charlie, Julia

REFLECTIONS:

Marriage is ordained by God and should be entered into reverently and through His guidance. If you are married, pray for your spouse every day—that you may love them as God intends.

Pray that they would know your love for them. If you are single, pray for God's divine leading as He brings the perfect person into your life.

CHAPTER 32

FAITH ADVENTURES IN VILSECK AND GRAFENVER MILITARY CHAPEL

Are they (angels) not all ministering spirits sent out to minister to those who will inherit salvation?

Hebrews 1:14

IN 2010, WE FELT CALLED to our third faith adventure in Germany. We had been alerted about the need for a Pentecostal military fellowship in Vilseck, Germany. Upon arriving, God helped us to secure a perfect apartment in the scenic town of Kemnot. Back in 2006, when we left Germany, we stored some basic furniture, bedroom furniture, office furniture, a lovely dining set and chairs, dishes, and items we needed for start-up, anticipating a quick return.

We soon found out the storage company had gone bankrupt, and we lost contact with our furniture. There was only one name and a telephone number available. Four years had gone by; we had not heard anything about our furniture or paid any storage costs. Finally, we called the number and obtained an office address.

In faith, we traveled from Vilseck to Ramstein only to discover no one was there. While praying in our car, we asked God what to do next. It was a somber feeling to think that perhaps our furniture was totally lost. However, it seemed we had no recourse in the natural but to drive the four hours back to our empty apartment.

As we were praying, a sharp-looking lady in a red suit appeared on the sidewalk. I immediately jumped out of our car and asked her about the name we had, telling her that we had come to pick up our furniture. She dug in her purse and said, "Oh, I have a key."

Then she said, "Follow me."

She put the top down on her VW convertible, and we sped through the countryside until arriving at a large warehouse. I remember thinking, *"This is not where we left the furniture!"*

She opened the massive sliding door and pointed to our furniture, which was haphazardly piled on the floor. We were overjoyed to identify our belongings. When we turned around to thank her, she was gone. We ran outside, but there was no one and no car in sight! Hebrews 1:14 talks about servant angels sent to care for God's people.

When we turned around to thank her, she was gone.

Later, we reminisced that she had not offered her name or relationship with the name on the storage contract. We quickly rented a truck, retrieved our belongings, and set up our charming apartment, knowing we had encountered an angel—up close and personal. This provision gave us great confidence that we were in God's will and right on track in Vilseck.

In God's providence, we had a divine appointment with Chaplin. Lt. Colonel Paul Lasley. He was so gracious to us and immediately took us under his care. He gave us the use of his chapel and co-sponsored all of our activities. As a result, many people came to Christ and received the Baptism in the Holy Spirit. Miracles of God's provision and blessing were everywhere.

At this juncture of the war in Iraq, we were losing many soldiers. Chaplin Lasley would preach numerous memorial services each week. I remember him asking us to be at every service just to pray for him. He preached powerfully and shared the gospel of a living salvation. The German army from the area was always there. I am sure they must have been moved by the powerful messages! Afterward, we would minister to the families.

OUR PRECIOUS SOLDIERS RETURNING HOME

Colossians 3:23-24, *"And whatever you do, do it heartily as for the Lord and not for men. Knowing that from the Lord you will receive the reward of the inheritance for you serve the Lord Christ."*

One of the unique joys of serving at Vilseck was when the troops would come home to their families. First, they would march into the gymnasium, assemble into formation, and stand at attention while the commanding officer would give commendations. Then, at the precise moment, he released them, the wives and kids would flood the gym floor into the arms of our soldiers, their husbands, dads, etc.

It was a very emotional scene and a time when Sheryl and I would spring into action. It quickly became apparent that some soldiers had no one to welcome them back. So we would make a beeline to these particular soldiers, thanking them for their service and giving a small gift to each one.

We enjoyed striking up conversations with them and praying with those who showed an interest. It was a great honor, and we took pleasure in ministering to our fantastic soldiers. We will always cherish these times of joy and pride in our incredible country—the United States of America.

REFLECTIONS:

Being a follower of Jesus means being a servant. It means praying for the lost and ministering to the lonely. Servanthood requires humility before the Lord. And, we have to make ourselves available to be the hands of Jesus in any situation.

Romans 12:15 says, "Morn with those who morn. Rejoice with those who rejoice." (NIV) Our calling is to quietly and faithfully do good works for the Kingdom of God. Every day we should be mindful of God's call for us. And be ready to serve Him by serving others.

FIFTY YEARS OF JOYFUL SERVICE TOGETHER IN MINISTRY

For the Lord God is a sun and shield, the Lord will give favor and glory, for no good thing will he withhold from the one who walks uprightly. Oh Lord of hosts, blessed is the man who rests in you.

Psalm 84:11-12

AS WE LOOK BACK at fifty-five years of wonderful marriage and over fifty years of serving the Lord, we are reminded of Joshua 23:14: *Not one thing has failed of all the good things which the Lord your God promised concerning you.* (AMP)

I often think back to my simple prayer as a teenager, when I told God I wanted to spend my life with that joyful girl. Sheryl has never lost her joy and has always been my sparkplug and my best friend.

Regularly, I tell her that I am eternally indebted to her for encouraging me to enter into full-time ministry. And for her being willing to share these faith adventures with me. She continues to be the love of my life—perhaps now, more than ever before.

Life is so good. And we continue to look forward to how God is going to surprise and bless us next. Someone said, "It's not over 'til Jesus comes, and then it's just the beginning!"

www.ingramcontent.com/pod-product-compliance
Lightning Source LLC
LaVergne TN
LVHW051059080426
835508LV00019B/1967